Publications of the
MINNESOTA HISTORICAL SOCIETY

RUSSELL W. FRIDLEY
Director and Editor

JUNE DRENNING HOLMQUIST
Associate Editor

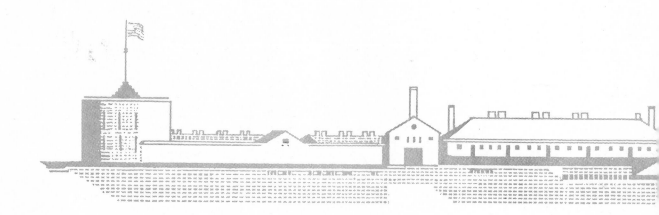

A Pictorial

THE
THIRTY-SECOND
STATE

History of Minnesota

BY BERTHA L. HEILBRON

ST. PAUL · THE MINNESOTA HISTORICAL SOCIETY · 1958

For some descendants of

KALMON *and* DINA LION

Minnesota pioneers of 1856

Preface

THIS BOOK represents an attempt to integrate pictorial and factual material about the Minnesota country from the mid-seventeenth century, when the earliest French explorers began to record their impressions of the area, to 1958, when the American commonwealth that took root and grew in this land of lakes and streams marked its centennial as the thirty-second state. In the resulting survey, I have emphasized visual, rather than written, sources. The accompanying narrative is intended to serve merely as a background for the pictures — an explanatory text that helps to give meaning and continuity to the almost five hundred illustrations here assembled for the first time within the covers of a single volume.

To present them to the best possible advantage, I have arranged in chronological sequence the diversified pictorial records relating to events from 1654 to about 1858, and have treated topically those reflecting the developments that marked a century of statehood. The texts of the chronological chapters are based largely on earlier state histories and previously published articles. Information for the topical discussions, on the other hand, has been drawn from widely varied sources, ranging from government documents and reports, newspapers, periodicals, and business records, to ephemeral pamphlets and leaflets. Thus the later chapters bring together much material that can be found in no other single work on Minnesota. Names of artists or photographers, dates whenever possible, and sources are included in the brief descriptive captions that accompany each illustration. All pictures not otherwise credited are from the collections of the Minnesota Historical Society.

In general, pictures were selected for their historical, rather than aesthetic, value. The choice of illustrations has been a personal matter, strongly influenced by my own tastes and interests. Some topics have been neglected or overlooked because they cannot be readily illustrated; others were omitted because visual sources are inadequate or uninteresting. Many a reader will doubtless miss pictures relating to favorite subjects that he would have stressed and perhaps treated in some detail. Complete coverage, however, could not be achieved in a single volume.

The publication of this selection from a mass of largely unexploited pictorial sources has given me an opportunity to express an interest which has been taking shape and expanding for almost three decades. The idea for this work evolved over the years as other members of the Minnesota Historical Society staff and I had occasion to examine the pictorial holdings of libraries, museums, and historical societies in the Twin Cities, Duluth, and many smaller Minnesota communities, and to cull out Minnesota materials in the collections assembled by the State Historical Society of Wisconsin in Madison, the Newberry Library and the Chicago Historical Society in Chicago, the City Art Museum and the Missouri Historical Society in St. Louis, and other Midwestern depositories. Late in 1954, at the suggestion of Dr. Solon J. Buck, I went to Washington, D.C., and New York for the purpose of finding and making an inventory of significant Minnesota pictures in the National Archives and other collections located in those centers. The rich lodes of pictorial records uncovered pointed up the possibilities for drawing together illustrations from the collections of the Minnesota Historical Society and other institutions in a visual review of the state's history. In 1956 the society's director, Russell W. Fridley, asked me to undertake such a work for publication in Minnesota's statehood centennial year, 1958.

Picture-hunting trips followed to Winnipeg in the autumn of 1956 and to Toronto, Ottawa, Montreal, Boston, New Haven, New York, and Washington, D.C., in the spring of 1957. Many of the thirty-odd museums, libraries, galleries, and other collecting agencies surveyed on those journeys and in 1954 yielded material for this book. They are among the eighty-three "Picture Sources" enumerated on pages 295 and 296. It was, of course, impossible to see and examine personally all the collections represented. Some contacts were made by telephone, and others by correspondence. Among the institutions approached by letter only were some sixty county and community historical societies in Minnesota. Hundreds of pictures that could not be included in the published work were assembled. They have been added to the society's permanent picture collection, which has acquired some unique new holdings as a result of the present publication project.

To pay for photographic reproductions of pictures of Minnesota interest and value that I located elsewhere, the late Carl W. Jones of Minneapolis provided special funds. I am deeply grateful to him for his generous contribution to the collecting phase of my undertaking, as well as for his support of a more extensive project looking toward the complete cataloging of the society's pictorial holdings. The progress of that work, which he initiated and organized, and which he joined with some twoscore other good friends of the society in financing, greatly simplified my use of the complicated files in the society's picture department.

Many others have contributed substantially to the preparation of this book. For special favors I wish to thank Clifford P. Wilson of the Hudson's Bay Company at Winnipeg, who gave me access to the pictorial files he had accumulated as editor of *The Beaver* and suggested many new avenues of research; Mrs. F. W. Gerber of Plainview, Miss Gertrude Gove of St. Cloud, and Mrs. Bunn T. Willson of Rochester, all of whom reassembled for my benefit pictures used earlier in local centennial pamphlets; and the Misses Anna E. R. and Laura Furness of St. Paul, who placed at my disposal portraits of members of the Ramsey family and their many friends. John Dobie of the Minnesota conservation department, Evan Hart of Milwaukee, Harold McCracken of Douglaston, Long Island, New York, and Sister Grace McDonald of the College of St. Benedict at St. Joseph are among those who supplied illuminating material on topics that might otherwise have been neglected.

Numerous librarians and curators connected with widely distributed institutions gave freely of their time and energy. Although the collections over which they preside are listed here, I should be negligent if I failed to acknowledge the many courtesies received from Miss Virginia Daiker of the prints and photographs division in the Library of Congress; Miss Josephine Cobb of the still picture department and Herman Friis of the cartographic records section in the National Archives; Pierre Brunet, assistant archivist, and A. E. H. Petrie of the picture department in the Public Archives of Canada; Hartwell Bowsfield, provincial archivist of Manitoba; Beaumont Newhall, curator of the George Eastman House; Mrs. Mary Frances Rhymer, curator of prints on the staff of the Chicago Historical Society; Father Thomas J. Shanahan of the St. Paul Seminary; Roy Swanson, librarian of the *St. Paul Dispatch-Pioneer Press*; Robert Hoag, chief reference librarian of the St. Paul Public Library; and Miss Betty Engebretson and Mrs. Martha Bray of the Minneapolis Athenaeum staff in the Minneapolis Public Library.

Dean Merrill E. Jarchow of Carleton College, chairman of the society's publications committee, and Professor Maude L. Lindquist of the history faculty in the University of Minnesota Duluth Branch read the manuscript and critically appraised chapters dealing with their special fields of interest. Professor Floyd O. Flom of the department of political science on the main campus of the University of Minnesota evaluated my review of political developments during a century of statehood, and Mrs. Rhoda Gilman provided an inspired title for the resulting chapter.

The enthusiastic co-operation of my colleagues on the staff of the Minnesota Historical Society, who gave me the advantage of their special skills and knowledge, has earned my eternal gratitude. For the opportunity to devote undivided energy to the preparation of this book, I am indebted to Mr. Fridley, who freed me from my usual editorial responsibilities from October, 1956, to March, 1958. Mrs. June Drenning Holmquist, associate editor, not only volunteered to take over the editorship of *Minnesota History* for an indefinite period, but she ably edited *The Thirty-second State*, rescued me from many a pitfall that marred early versions of the manuscript, and piloted the book through the press with the assistance of Mrs. Jean Brookins. Eugene D. Becker, curator of pictures, and his assistant, Mrs. Helene Thomson, were untiring in their efforts to find for my use the very best among the 450,000 pictures under their stewardship. I wish especially to thank Mr. Becker for preparing hundreds of photographic prints of high quality for reproduction in this volume. James Taylor Dunn, the society's librarian, generously shared with me his store of information and his collection of pictures on the St. Croix Valley. Miss Lois M. Fawcett maintained her reputation as the most helpful of reference librarians by digging out bits of obscure information as they were needed. Miss Lucile M. Kane, curator of manuscripts, and F. Sanford Cutler, former museum curator, read and criticized chapters relating, respectively, to economic and Indian history. Chester Kozlak of the museum staff prepared the maps. Mrs. Ilse Levi, a part-time editorial assistant, did much of the basic research for the later chapters, and she compiled the index. Mrs. Phyllis Sandstrom patiently and cheerfully typed uncounted revisions of the manuscript. Without the assistance of these and other fellow workers, this book could not have been carried to completion.

BERTHA L. HEILBRON

MINNESOTA HISTORICAL SOCIETY
    October, 1958

Contents

PART II

A Century of Statehood
1858-1958

PART I

From Unexplored Wilderness
to Frontier Territory

1654
1858

1.

The Fleur-de-lis
on Western Waters

WHEN MINNESOTA was admitted to the Union in 1858, it added a thirty-second star to the American flag and a musical name to the list of states. The white man gave the new political entity a name long used by the Indian to designate a tributary of the Mississippi. Its meaning in translation—sky-tinted waters—has a wider implication, for Minnesota has within its borders more water than any other American commonwealth. Located in the center of the North American continent, the state can boast a square mile of water for every twenty of land, or a total water area of more than four thousand square miles, excluding Lake Superior. Minnesota's lakes, many of them still uncounted and unmapped, number well over eleven thousand. They drain into three great river systems that carry Minnesota-born waters to as many seas.

Largest among Minnesota's streams is the Mississippi, which cuts a wide swath southward through the heart of the continent on its way to salt water. Only a stone's throw from the source of the Father of Waters in Lake Itasca are lakes that drain into tributaries of the northward-flowing Red River. Its waters empty into Lake Winnipeg before reaching Hudson Bay and the Arctic. Flowing into Lake Superior from the Arrowhead country of northeastern Minnesota are scores of little streams carrying waters that make their way to the Atlantic through the eastward-moving Great Lakes-St. Lawrence system. Between the spots where these streams with their far-flung destinations originate are heights of land—areas from which the waters flow in two and sometimes three directions. Although they rise only slightly above the surrounding districts, they are, like the imposing Rocky Mountains, true continental divides. A land of placid lakes, of streams fanning out in three directions, of hardly perceptible divides—that was the Minnesota country in 1650, that is Minnesota today.

More than any other geographic feature of the Northland, Minnesota's waterways influenced its history. They determined the course of exploration, of trade, of settlement, of transportation, of economic growth, and they outline large portions of three of the state's four boundaries. The rivers began to play their part in shaping Minnesota's future in the mid-seventeenth century, when the land and its heaven-reflecting waters were still unknown to Europeans. Any white men who may have seen the area earlier failed to report their findings and therefore cannot qualify as discoverers. It remained for a few venturesome Frenchmen not only to find, but to make known, the country in the center of North America where the waters divide.

These subjects of Louis XIV set out from the colony of New France on the lower reaches of the St. Lawrence River in eastern Canada. By way of a mythical Northwest Passage, the adventurous explorers of the seventeenth century dreamed of reaching the Western Sea and finding the riches of Cathay. What they were seeking as they carried the Fleur-de-lis of their homeland westward actually lay far beyond the continental limits of North America. As they were lured ever farther inland, the mystery of North America's vast fresh-water seas—the Great Lakes—began to unfold. Samuel de Champlain found Lakes Huron and Ontario in 1615, and in 1634 Jean Nicolet penetrated to the west coast of Lake Michigan. Convinced that he had reached the Far East, he stepped ashore arrayed in an elaborate Oriental robe only to be welcomed by North American Indians.

Another decade dawned before the largest of the Great Lakes—Superior, which borders on Minnesota—was added to the map in 1641. Via its waters a pair of fur traders, Pierre Radisson and his brother-in-law, Médard Chouart, sieur des Groseilliers, voyaged westward in 1654 and pushed inland from its south shore. Just where they went and what they saw between that year and 1660 is somewhat uncertain, since Radisson's account of their adventures reflects the era's confused impressions of Midwest geography. He makes it clear, however, that he and Groseilliers came into contact with the Minnesota Sioux and learned much about their way of life. Some historians believe that these French traders went as far as Prairie Island in the Mississippi River near Hastings before returning to New France. There they quarreled with the governor. The argument was to have far-reaching results, since it caused the brothers-in-law to desert the French and obtain British support for their trading and exploring operations. One outcome of their shift in loyalty was the organization in 1670 of the Hudson's Bay Company, which is still active in the North American fur trade.

The explorations of Radisson and Groseilliers reflect two objectives in the westward push of the French—the expansion of the domain of Louis XIV and the search for wealth in furs. The activities of the Jesuits and other Catholic missionaries who early joined the movement toward the West give evidence of a third objective. These courageous friars saw in the new lands an opportunity to expand the influence of the church by carrying its word to the red men. One of them, Father Jacques Marquette, and a layman named Louis Jolliet left Mackinac at the western end of Lake Huron in June, 1673, crossed Lake Michigan to Green Bay, pushed up the Fox River, portaged to the Wisconsin, and in time floated out upon the waters of the Mississippi. With the current they drifted as far as the mouth of the Arkansas, proving that the Father of Waters flows southward. To them belongs the credit for discovering the upper Mississippi.

4

RADISSON AND GROSEILLIERS, pictured on western waters, may well have been the earliest Europeans to see the Minnesota country. Radisson is represented standing and Groseilliers seated. *Reproduction of a painting by Frederic Remington, in* Collier's, January 13, 1906; *courtesy Harold McCracken.*

Du LUTH, his voyageurs, and his Indian guides are shown landing at Fond du Lac, at the head of Lake Superior, in the summer of 1679. *Oil by Francis Lee Jaques, about 1922; courtesy Minnesota Arrowhead Association, Duluth.*

FATHER LOUIS HENNEPIN attained a major place in the story of Minnesota exploration in 1680, when he and Auguelle discovered the falls at the site of Minneapolis. The oil reproduced below, dated 1694, is the only known likeness of the adventurous friar who was among the earliest explorers of the upper Missisippi. The portrait was once owned by James J. Hill.

THE FALLS OF ST. ANTHONY were named by Father Hennepin for his patron saint, Anthony of Padua. The view above, picturing Hennepin and Auguelle discovering the cataract, was painted by George Catlin against a background he first saw in 1835, when it still looked much as it did in the Belgian friar's day. This is one of twenty-six oils depicting the adventures of La Salle and his followers which Catlin painted for Louis Philippe of France and delivered just before the Revolution of 1848. The artist never was paid for his work and eventually he recovered the pictures. *Courtesy American Museum of Natural History, New York*

6

Another seeker for new lands and the riches they might hold was Daniel Greysolon, sieur du Luth. Hoping that he would eventually reach the Pacific, he set out for the West by way of the Great Lakes in 1678, reached Fond du Lac, at the head of the lakes near the city that bears his name, in the following summer, and then pushed his way inland to a great Sioux village on Mille Lacs Lake, where he laid claim to the area in the name of the French king. After returning to Lake Superior for the winter, Du Luth resumed his exploring activities by following the Bois Brulé and St. Croix rivers to the Mississippi. There he heard that some of his countrymen were in the vicinity, held captive by the Sioux. Du Luth decided to find them, and on July 25, 1680, he came upon Father Louis Hennepin, Antoine Auguelle, and Michael Accault with a hunting party of Indians. The great French pathfinder La Salle had sent them from his Illinois fort to explore the upper Mississippi, and somewhere below Lake Pepin they had been captured by a Sioux war party. They were taken to the Mille Lacs village, where they were held for several months before Father Hennepin and Auguelle obtained leave to go down the Mississippi on an excursion

7

THE MISSION OF ST. MICHAEL THE ARCHANGEL, established at Fort Beauharnois in 1727, probably was the first Christian church on Minnesota soil. *Anonymous pencil sketch; courtesy St. Paul Seminary, St. Paul.*

TREMPEALEAU, on the east bank of the Mississippi, was the site of one of the many French posts in the upper valley of that stream. It was occupied from 1731 to 1736. *Drawing by Mrs. Hettie M. Pierce; courtesy State Historical Society of Wisconsin, Madison.*

which resulted in the discovery of the Falls of St. Anthony early in July. Some weeks later, while the venturesome friar and his two companions were hunting with a band of Sioux, Du Luth found them, forced the Indians to release them, and gave up his own exploring plans to return with them to Mackinac.

Two years after sending Father Hennepin and his companions to the upper Mississippi, La Salle descended the great river to its mouth and claimed all the territory it drained—Louisiana—for Louis XIV and France. Further exploration of the river's upper reaches followed, and trading posts were founded throughout the area. Before long about twenty establishments on northern waterways gave evidence of occupation under the Fleur-de-lis. Among them were Fort St. Antoine, built on the east shore of Lake Pepin by Nicolas Perrot in 1686, and Fort L'Huillier established in 1700 by Pierre Charles le Sueur at the mouth of the Blue Earth on the river for which Minnesota is named. That eastward-flow-

THE CHEVALIER de la VERENDRYE led an exloring party westward beyond the Missouri in 1743, penetrating perhaps as far as the foothills of the Rockies, but more likely only to the Black Hills, where he encountered Indians who used horses. *Reproduction of a painting by Remington, in Collier's, February 10, 1906; courtesy Mr. McCracken.*

A LEAD PLATE, dated March 30, 1743, was deposited by members of the La Vérendrye expedition of that year. It was recovered in 1913 on a hill near Fort Pierre, South Dakota. The original is owned by the South Dakota State Historical Society at Pierre.

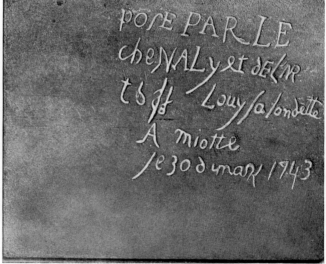

9

ing stream may well have been explored as early as 1688–89 by another Frenchman, the Baron de Lahontan; some believe that his Long River was none other than the Minnesota. Still more French posts were established on Lake Pepin in the first half of the eighteenth century. Fort Beauharnois, built near the present site of Frontenac in 1727 by the Sieur de la Perrière, was named for the governor general of Canada. Its log stockade, twelve feet high, surrounded an enclosure a hundred feet square.

Far to the north, on the Northwest Angle of the Lake of the Woods, Pierre Gaultier de Varennes, sieur de la Vérendrye, raised the Fleur-de-lis over still another Minnesota post. This was Fort St. Charles, built in 1732 and occupied for more than two decades on what, until the admission of Alaska in 1958, was the northernmost point in the United States. A burning desire to blaze a trail to the Western Sea prompted La Vérendrye to organize an expedition of some fifty men, including three of his sons and his nephew, to explore the country west of the Great Lakes. These Frenchmen not only penetrated beyond the Missouri, but they built a chain of posts, of which Fort St. Charles was one, stretching from Rainy Lake along northward-flowing waters as far as the Saskatchewan country. Misfortune plagued La Vérendrye; his nephew died, and his eldest son as well as Father Jean-Pierre Aulneau, a Jesuit priest who went with him to Fort St. Charles, and nineteen of his voyageurs were murdered by Sioux Indians. Nevertheless the elder La Vérendrye continued his efforts to explore the West until he died in 1749. With the death of this courageous pathfinder, the era of French exploration in the center of North America came to a close. Although they failed to find the Western Sea, the subjects of Louis XIV added Lake Superior, the upper Mississippi, and the lakes that mark the Canadian boundary to the map of the Minnesota country.

A BUFFALO, as pictured in Hennepin's book.

2.

Exploring under the Union Jack

MINNESOTA'S THREE GREAT WATERWAYS passed from the control of France to that of England and Spain shortly after 1760. The domination of the Fleur-de-lis in North America came to an end with the victory of the Union Jack in the French and Indian War. Under the terms of the treaty which marked the close of the conflict in 1763, Great Britain acquired all Canada east of the Father of Waters, as well as the right to free navigation of that stream. West of the Mississippi, the French lost the lands they had discovered by ceding them to Spain in 1762. The Spaniards, who retained their sway during four decades, had little or no influence on the area. The British, on the other hand, though they ruled only half as long, left an indelible mark in the land of sky-tinted waters. They continued the westward push initiated by the French.

The influence of the Union Jack penetrated the Minnesota area through a line of men who went west first to trade with the Indians and incidentally to explore. This combination of interests gave a distinctly commercial flavor to late eighteenth-century exploration in the Northland. One of the earliest, as well as one of the most widely known, of the English trading explorers was Jonathan Carver, a native of Massachusetts who dreamed of continuing the old search for the Northwest Passage and the Western Sea. In 1766 he followed the Mississippi northward from a post at Prairie du Chien, near the mouth of the Wisconsin, to the Falls of St. Anthony. After spending much of the following winter busily trading with the Indians in the Minnesota River Valley, he attended a council held by the red men in the spring of 1767 at a great cave overlooking the Mississippi within the present limits of St. Paul. The cavern has since been known as Carver's Cave.

In Carver's wake came a group of traders who added to the knowledge of the Minnesota country while working for one of the great English companies organized to trade with the Indians. The most powerful of these firms were the Hudson's Bay and the North West companies. A bitter rivalry between them dominated the fur trade and

11

JONATHAN CARVER was the first trading explorer to follow the Mississippi into the Minnesota country under the British flag. *Frontispiece from Carver's* Travels *(London, 1781).*

THIS SKETCH OF CARVER'S CAVE was made by Robert Ormsby Sweeny on May 1, 1867, when members of the Minnesota Historical Society celebrated the centennial of the explorer's visit to the upper Mississippi country.

THE FALLS OF ST. ANTHONY were pictured in a volume of *Travels* which Carver wrote in England after his trip to the West. It was translated into several languages and appeared in many editions. Carver's picture, first published in 1778, is the earliest known view of the cataract.

exploration of the late eighteenth and early nineteenth centuries. Among the exploring traders who combined searching for new lands with harvesting furs were Alexander Henry, the elder, and his nephew, Alexander Henry, the younger. The former began to trade out of Mackinac as early as 1763, and he was still active more than a decade later along what became Minnesota's northern boundary; the latter traded farther to the west in the valley of the Red River. At Pembina, near the point where the border cuts across that stream, the younger Henry built a post just after the turn of the century, in 1801. He was associated with the North West Company, which controlled the fur trade of the area that became Minnesota from 1783 until after the War of 1812.

Connected with the same firm was David Thompson, a pioneering geographer of the first rank who explored westward from Lake Superior. He had been employed for fourteen years by the Hudson's Bay Company, but when the Nor'Westers in 1797 offered him an opportunity to survey and map their vast trading area, he transferred his allegiance. In the years that followed, with headquarters at Grand Portage, he explored the hitherto largely unknown wilderness stretching beyond Lake Superior to the Pacific while collecting furs for his company. His journeys resulted in the first de-

13

tailed and accurate map of the American Northwest, which earned him a reputation, among scientists of a later day, as one of the greatest geographers of all time. As late as 1823, Thompson helped survey the boundary between the United States and Canada westward from Grand Portage to the Lake of the Woods.

Another trading map maker who knew Minnesota's waterways at firsthand during the British regime was a Connecticut Yankee named Peter Pond. From 1773 to 1775 he conducted extensive trading operations with the Minnesota Indians from a post, probably near Lac qui Parle, on the St. Peter's or Minnesota River. His headquarters during these years, however, were at Prairie du Chien, which had been Carver's stopping place in the previous decade. There, until after the War of 1812, the Union Jack floated over an important post known for a time as Fort McKay. One of Pond's maps probably was used by Benjamin Franklin in 1783 during negotiations for the treaty of Paris at the close of the American Revolution, indicating the importance of the cartographic contributions made by this and other venturesome traders.

During the years of British supremacy in the Minnesota country, both the North West and the Hudson's Bay companies had posts along the waterways that mark the boundary between Minnesota and Canada. From Grand Portage and later Fort William, their stockaded forts stretched westward, south as well as north of the border. Among them were posts on Basswood Lake, Rainy Lake, Lake of the Woods, Roseau Lake, and on the Red River in the vicinity of Pembina and at the mouth of the Assiniboine. Upper and Lower Fort Garry, both on the Red River well north of the border, became important centers of trade for the Hudson's Bay Company. A third British firm, the XY Company, also had establishments in some of these localities, like Rainy Lake and Pembina.

The North West Company built at least twenty-four posts in the Minnesota region. Included were establishments at Fond du Lac, at Leech and Sandy lakes, and on the Red River. Most important, however, was the great fur post known as Grand Portage on Lake Superior just below the present international boundary. There each July hundreds of traders gathered. Some came from Montreal, bringing trade goods and supplies; others arrived from the interior with cargoes of rich pelts gathered while wintering in the wilderness. Furs, trade goods, and supplies had to be carried over a nine-mile portage between the lakeside post and Fort Charlotte inland on the Pigeon River. The trail avoided the long series of waterfalls and rapids that prohibit navigation on the stream's lower reaches. Grand Portage was the gateway to the wilderness, the starting point for every trading expedition that followed the much-used Pigeon River route to the interior. Their role in the frontier history of Minnesota is commemorated in a national monument established by Congress in 1958. It includes not only the sites of Grand Portage and Fort Charlotte, but the course of the portage trail between them.

With the close of the Revolutionary War, under the terms of the treaty of 1783, much of the trading area extending westward from Lake Superior became part of the new United States. Among the posts that changed their national affiliations was Grand

FORT McKAY at Prairie du Chien was the scene of this ceremony in 1814, when the Indians gathered about the Union Jack to welcome a British army officer from Mackinac. *Water color by Peter Rindisbacher, about 1825; courtesy McCord National Museum, McGill University, Montreal.*

THE SANDY LAKE POST was one of a group established by the North West Company after 1792 to exploit the rich fur resources of the Minnesota country. Later, in the 1820s, the American Fur Company established a post in the area. *Idealized sketch by Evan A. Hart, based on excavations of the site, 1956.*

GRAND PORTAGE, the principal post of the North West Company from 1783 to 1804, consisted of sixteen buildings enclosed by a stockade. The firm had its own ship of ninety-five tons, which sailed via the Great Lakes between Montreal and the post on Lake Superior. *From Joseph Bouchette,* Map of the Provinces of Upper and Lower Canada *(1815); courtesy Ontario Department of Public Records and Archives, Toronto.*

FORT WILLIAM became the leading British post on Lake Superior after Grand Portage was abandoned in 1804 and traders began to use the Kaministikwia River route to the interior in place of that via the Pigeon River. *Water color dated 1812; courtesy Lieutenant Colonel S. A. Heward, Toronto, and the Hudson's Bay Company, Winnipeg.*

Portage. With the route via the Pigeon River, it was abandoned by the British in 1804, despite the fact that traders for the North West and Hudson's Bay companies continued to operate on both sides of the international boundary until 1816. In that year the fur trade south of the Canadian border ended for the British, because Congress passed an act providing that only American citizens could be licensed to trade with the Indians in the United States. The North West Company, cut off from its American sources of furs, declined in power as well as in wealth. Before long, it was forced to merge with its traditional rival, the Hudson's Bay Company. Their union in 1821 marked the end of a long period of conflict which at times broke into open warfare. The victorious firm continued to operate north of the border, where until 1870 it had not only commercial but political authority.

Fort William replaced Grand Portage as the chief trading emporium on the north shore of Lake Superior. It was near the site of a post built by Du Luth at the mouth of the Kaministikwia River in 1679, and it utilized a route to the west long known to the French. The new fort retained its major role in the fur trade after the competing North West and Hudson's Bay companies merged. The city that grew up on the site of Fort William is still a center for this wilderness business—a symbol of British influence both north and south of the border in the wide area that extends westward from Lake Superior to the Rocky Mountains.

3.

Traders' Frontier

BY THE TIME the British withdrew from the Minnesota country, its three important waterways and many of the lakes that feed them were dotted with trading posts. Scores were built by French, British, and, later, by American traders; it is definitely known that more than a hundred and thirty flourished in Minnesota and near its borders in adjoining states and Canada. They were centers of big business in the wilderness —big at least by the standards of the day. Across the counters of the trading stores, transactions that often ran into five figures were conducted each year. There the Indians exchanged the furs they collected for blankets, guns, ammunition, brightly colored fabrics, kettles, knives, tobacco, trinkets, beads, and other trade goods. The red man paid for such items at greatly inflated rates. For a tin kettle worth about $2.50, for example, he was obliged to give sixty rats valued at $12.00. The skins of muskrats, which were more numerous than other animals trapped by the Indians, were virtually a medium of exchange in the fur trade, especially after beaver skins, long used as a unit of value, became scarce in the Minnesota country.

After the British left, the posts and outfits located on Minnesota's waterways south of the boundary were taken over by John Jacob Astor's American Fur Company, which had been chartered in 1808. This concern built new posts on many of the sites long exploited by the British companies. An example is Pembina, where there was an American trading establishment as early as 1824. Others sprang up across northern Minnesota throughout the decade of the 1820s, and soon Americans were operating from such points in the wilderness as Lake Winnibigoshish, Red, Cass, Leech, Sandy, and Gull lakes, and the Crow Wing River. Farther south, about 1820, the American Fur Company opened its headquarters for trade with the Sioux at Mendota, where the Minnesota meets the Mississippi. Subordinate posts along the former stream included those at Traverse des Sioux, Little Rock, Lac qui Parle, and Lake Traverse. Another American concern, the Columbia Fur Company, also operated in this vicinity.

THE TYPICAL VOYAGEUR, as portrayed above, smoked a clay pipe and dressed warmly during the winter in a heavy blue capote topped by a red cap. *Oil by Mrs. Samuel B. Abbe, probably painted in the 1850s.*

VOYAGEUR FRED FARIBAULT is pictured at the right in summer garb, which included a short shirt, flowing scarf, deerskin leggings, moccasins, and multicolored sash, from which hung a gay, beaded tobacco pouch. *Sketch by Frank B. Mayer, 1851; courtesy New York Public Library.*

Despite the shifts in management and in national affiliations that marked the fur trade in the decades from 1760 to 1820, methods and even personnel changed little on Minnesota's lakes and rivers. The French-Canadian voyageurs remained in the area after the French regime ended, continuing under the Union Jack and the Stars and Stripes the specialized work that made them so essential to this wilderness business. Skilled especially as canoemen, the voyageurs were usually short and stocky, with overdeveloped shoulders and thin legs. These men could sit day after day in canoes, which they managed with equal skill on the rough waters of inland seas like Lake Superior or in the erratic rapids of wildly tumbling streams; they could carry enormous loads over the often rough and difficult portage trails that skirted cataracts or served as links between lakes; they could thrive for months on a monotonous diet of dried corn and pemmican, a mixture of buffalo meat and fat that could be easily transported.

19

NORTH CANOES, which were rarely more than twenty-five feet in length, required crews of only eight voyageurs, as compared with fourteen for the Montreal canoes. The smaller craft were generally used on the maze of streams and lakes in the vast wilderness stretching westward from Lake Superior both in Minnesota and Canada. *Colored engraving after a painting by Frances Anne Hopkins, about 1870.*

Over well-defined routes, the voyageurs pushed inland from Lake Superior, up the Mississippi, or down the Red. The three directions taken by Minnesota's waterways were familiar to these sons of the wilderness. Their moccasined feet wore deep trails over the land between the eastward-moving Bois Brulé and the southward-flowing St. Croix; between the St. Louis River and the creeks flowing into Sandy Lake; between Lakes Big Stone and Traverse; as well as around drops in elevation like the high falls of the Pigeon and the St. Louis rivers. It was the voyageurs, too, who built the stockaded posts in the wilderness where they and their employers—partners or clerks connected with the great trading companies—passed the long, dreary, northern winters. Every trip to the interior by canoe and portage had as its objective a trading post or fort, from which began also the return journeys eastward in the spring with the winter's fur harvest. The characteristics and accomplishments of the voyageurs, and their contributions to the arduous activities connected with Minnesota's first business, have been recounted in meticulous detail in a book by Grace Lee Nute. Pictured here are some of the activities that she describes.

The voyageurs were largely undisturbed by political changes in the Great Lakes and upper Mississippi areas. Their attachment was to a way of life in the wilderness rather than to a flag. Whether they were employed by the North West Company or the Ameri-

IN HUGE MONTREAL CANOES, thirty-five to forty feet long, skilled voyageurs transported men and supplies between Montreal and Grand Portage or Fort William, via the St. Lawrence River and the Great Lakes. The passengers here pictured are Edward M. Hopkins of the Hudson's Bay Company and his wife, Frances Anne, who painted this oil about 1870. *Courtesy Public Archives of Canada, Ottawa.*

can Fur Company was not of vital importance to these hardy French-speaking canoemen from eastern Canada. A few French Canadians, however, attained positions of leadership with British or American firms. There was, for example, Jean Baptiste Perrault, who went out to the head of the lakes in 1793 and built the North West Company's post at Fond du Lac. Both he and Jean Baptiste Cadotte were partners of the company in charge of the trade for an extensive section of what became Minnesota.

Some of the principal traders of the American period, too, were of French origin. Joseph Renville presided over the Columbia Fur Company's fort at Lac qui Parle; both Jean Baptiste Faribault and his son Alexander were prominent in the Minnesota Valley trade; Joseph Rolette was connected with the American Fur Company at Prairie du Chien, and his son of the same name traded at Pembina; Alexis Bailly had posts at Mendota and later at Wabasha; both Louis Provençalle and Joseph Laframboise traded in the Minnesota Valley. The Scotch, long active with the British trading companies, also played a part in the American trade; typical of this group were Martin McLeod and William Aitken. Later came wilderness entrepreneurs of English and Yankee descent, like Henry H. Sibley and Joseph R. Brown. These men of varied backgrounds built the traders' frontier in the Minnesota country, bridging the gap between the era of the explorer and the day of the settler.

THE VOYAGEURS carried canoes and baggage over well-defined, though often rough, portage trails that connected waterways or avoided rapids. Two men portaged the canoe, while the others carried trade goods or furs packed in bales weighing ninety pounds each. *Water color by William Armstrong, about 1870; courtesy William H. Coverdale Collection, Manoir Richelieu, Murray Bay, Quebec, and the Canada Steamship Lines, Montreal.*

THE END OF A PORTAGE was a place for resting, eating, smoking, and reloading the canoes. Note the packs marked "HB" for Hudson's Bay Company. Some voyageurs of unusual strength could carry three or four such packs. *Water color by Armstrong, about 1870; courtesy Coverdale Collection and the Canada Steamship Lines.*

WOODEN CROSSES, like this one at Island Portage on the Kaministikwia River, were erected by voyageurs in memory of companions who died in accidents. *Water color by George Back, 1826; courtesy Public Archives of Canada.*

STORES to which the Indians took the furs collected during the winter hunting and trapping season were a feature of every trading post. There in exchange they received the varied items that the white man had to offer, including firearms, traps, tobacco, and all too often whisky. To and from these wilderness business centers the voyageurs made their long and arduous canoe trips, transporting both trade goods and furs. *From Robert M. Ballantyne,* Hudson Bay: or, Everyday Life in the Wilds *(London, 1876).*

FOND du LAC became the site of an American Fur Company post in 1816, when the North West Company was obliged to evacuate an establishment built there earlier by Perrault. It was an important trading center until the American Fur Company failed in the 1840s. *From Thomas L. McKenney,* Sketches of a Tour to the Lakes *(Baltimore, 1827).*

MENDOTA at the mouth of the Minnesota River opposite Fort Snelling was the American Fur Company's chief depot for trade with the Sioux after 1819. It was never a stockaded post, consisting merely of a group of buildings clustered about a trading store. *Oil by Seth Eastman, probably painted in the 1840s; courtesy Thomas Gilcrease Institute of American History and Art, Tulsa, Oklahoma.*

PEMBINA near the international boundary on the Red River was the site of posts occupied after 1797 by the British North West, Hudson's Bay, and XY companies, and by the American Fur Company. The Hudson's Bay Company built this typical stockaded fort just north of the border. *Water color by W. H. E. Napier, 1858; courtesy Mrs. George S. Currie, Westmount, Quebec.*

UPPER FORT GARRY was a Hudson's Bay Company post at the junction of the Assiniboine and Red rivers, where Winnipeg is now located. Connecting the fort and Pembina with Minnesota markets on the Mississippi were the Red River trails, used in the 1840s and later by traders who transported their furs in wooden carts for sale at St. Paul and other early settlements. *From a lithograph showing the fort as it appeared in the 1860s; courtesy Hudson's Bay Company.*

4.

Sioux and Chippewa

JUST AS THE TRADERS depended upon the voyageurs to transport their goods and man their posts, they looked to the native red men of the Minnesota country to harvest the area's annual crop of furs. These were of great variety, including badger, coon, fisher, mink, marten, otter, bear, wolf, fox, and deer skins, as well as buffalo robes. Most important and numerous, however, were beaver and muskrat skins.

Most of the Minnesota Indians belonged to two tribes—the Chippewa or Ojibway and the Sioux or Dakota. When white men first penetrated the area, it was occupied largely by the Sioux, but by 1800 they had been forced out of their northern land of lakes and forests by the Chippewa. For more than a century before they invaded the land of the Sioux, the Chippewa had been trading with the white men, first in the St. Lawrence Valley and then in the Great Lakes region. Thus, by the time they fought their way into the Minnesota country, they were well equipped with the white man's firearms, steel knives, and tools. The Sioux, who still depended upon primitive spears and bows and arrows, were no match for the invaders. After decades of bloody warfare, the defeated tribe lost all its lands east of the Mississippi and north of the Crow Wing.

The two groups of red men remained traditional enemies, however, and their perpetual warfare hindered both the white man's fur trade and the later progress of settlement. Although numerous attempts were made to bring about peace between the warring tribes, the situation seemed only to grow worse. After a single agency was established for both at Fort Snelling in 1820, councils looking toward a settlement of their differences were held not only at the Minnesota post but at Prairie du Chien and even in the national capital. Such efforts met with little success. Raids, skirmishes, and attacks continued, with some of the more serious battles taking place in 1839 and 1842. As late as 1853, the long-standing enmity broke into open conflict on the streets of St. Paul. Until most of the Sioux were removed from the Minnesota area in the 1860s, it remained a red man's battleground.

26

THE GRAND COUNCIL of 1825, held at Fort Crawford, Prairie du Chien, represents an early attempt to bring about peace between the Sioux and Chippewa. Nearly four hundred Indians from the upper Mississippi met with white commissioners and agreed on a dividing line between tribal lands which was to be crossed only on peaceful errands. It extended diagonally through the Minnesota country from west to east, crossing the Mississippi about where St. Cloud now stands. Although representatives of the tribes smoked the calumet over the agreement, it did little to establish lasting peace between them. *Lithograph by James Otto Lewis, in his* Aboriginal Port Folio *(1835).*

Not only were the Sioux and the Chippewa perpetually at war, but their customs and habits differed sharply, presenting numerous contrasts. The Sioux lived in cone-shaped skin tipis in winter, and in bark huts in summer; the Chippewa built dome-like wigwams of birch bark. The Sioux were expert horsemen; the Chippewa traveled much by water in their skillfully constructed bark canoes. The Sioux placed their dead on scaffolds; the Chippewa buried their deceased kinsmen. These and other customs of the Minnesota Indians are illustrated in the pages that follow.

THE CHIPPEWA WIGWAM
usually was a dome-shaped
dwelling made of birch
bark stretched over a frame
of saplings. *Photograph tak-
en about 1870.*

GRAND PORTAGE became a Chippewa Indian village after the British withdrew from this once-
important post on Lake Superior. The type of bark hut pictured was adapted from the Sioux
tipi. The village still exists on what is now a Chippewa reservation. *Oil by Eastman Johnson,
1856; courtesy Hulbert Taft, Cincinnati.*

28

THE SIOUX TIPI was a cone-shaped dwelling made of skins over a framework of poles. Used chiefly as a winter shelter, it could be easily taken down and transported by nomadic Indians engaged in hunting buffalo or gathering furs.

KAPOSIA, near the present site of South St. Paul, was a typical Sioux village of semipermanent bark huts occupied chiefly in summer. It was also known as Little Crow's village for its chief. *Water color by Eastman, about 1850; courtesy James Jerome Hill Reference Library, St. Paul.*

WITHIN THE BARK LODGE of the Sioux, an elevated platform along three walls provided a place for sleeping, resting, and smoking. Cooking was done over a fire on a hearth in the center of the floor, and the smoke escaped through an opening in the roof. *Wash drawing by Sweeny, about 1852.*

BUFFALO HIDES cured and stretched by the Sioux women were used for covering tipis and making moccasins and other items of clothing. *Drawing by Sweeny, about 1852.*

THE MEDICINE MAN of the Sioux used rattles and mysterious concoctions in his attempts to drive from patients the evil spirits believed to cause illness. Most of these primitive doctors were members of a secret medicine society. *Drawing by Sweeny, about 1852.*

ANNUAL HUNTS on the Plains, where vast herds of buffaloes roamed, were a colorful and important feature of Sioux life. These Indians were dependent upon the buffalo for food, clothing, and shelter, as well as for hides bartered in the fur trade. *Water color by Alfred Jacob Miller, probably based on sketches made in 1837; courtesy Public Archives of Canada.*

EXPERT HORSEMANSHIP characterized the buffalo hunting of the Sioux, who usually rode without saddles and stirrups when attacking their prey. *Oil by John Mix Stanley, 1845; courtesy National Museum, Smithsonian Institution, Washington, D.C.*

WHEN THE SIOUX TRAVELED to new camps or hunting grounds, they used both their horses and their women as beasts of burden. Tipis, food, clothing, weapons, and furs were carried by the squaws or transported on horse-drawn travois. *Water color by Eastman, about 1850; courtesy Hill Reference Library.*

THE CHIPPEWA TRAVELED in family groups during the winter hunting season, using snowshoes and toboggans. Such trips were made in search of meat for food and furs that could be traded for guns and other goods. *Water color by Rindisbacher, about 1823; courtesy United States Military Academy, West Point.*

SPEARING MUSKRATS in winter provided the Indians with pelts that were of prime importance in the wilderness fur business. The value of trade goods was often reckoned in rat skins, and traders' accounts are filled with references to them. *Water color by Eastman, about 1850; courtesy Hill Reference Library.*

GATHERING WILD RICE provided the Chippewa with one of their main articles of food. These Indians, whose lives were closely associated with the waters of their native area, developed great skill in making birch-bark canoes like that pictured. *Water color by Eastman, about 1850; courtesy Hill Reference Library.*

THE SCALP DANCE of the Sioux followed the return of a successful war party, which doubtless went forth to kill Chippewa. This wild and savage dance was not only a kind of celebration, but a form of thanksgiving for victory over a hated and greatly feared enemy. Both men and women participated in scalp dances, though in separate ceremonies. *Wash drawing by Sweeny, 1862.*

THE SNOWSHOE DANCE of the Chippewa, which marked the year's first snowfall, was one of many Indian ceremonies occasioned by seasonal changes and weather conditions. Among others were the sun and thunder dances. *Oil by Catlin, about 1848; courtesy National Museum, Smithsonian Institution.*

THE GAME OF LACROSSE, which was highly competitive, was played with crooked sticks that were used to scoop up and throw a ball. Sioux Indians at Traverse des Sioux were competing against visitors from Kaposia in the game shown here. *Water color by Mayer, 1898; courtesy Goucher College, Baltimore.*

A SIOUX BALLPLAYER, holding his lacrosse stick in readiness for a game, wore only a breechcloth held in place by an elaborately decorated girdle. Ornaments of furs and feathers trailed behind the fleet player as he ran, adding to the colorful effect of the spectacle. *Oil by Catlin, about 1840; courtesy National Museum, Smithsonian Institution.*

BURIAL SCAFFOLDS were used by the Sioux, who wrapped their dead in skins or blankets and placed them with some of their earthly possessions on elevated platforms or in the branches of trees, beyond the reach of animals. Eventually, the bones were collected and buried. *Photograph by D. F. Barry, 1870.*

MINIATURE WIGWAMS or shelters marked the graves in which the Chippewa buried their dead. Inside the shelter, the Indians placed food and articles that might be useful in the hereafter. *Courtesy Public Archives of Manitoba, Winnipeg.*

36

5.

The Stars and Stripes Move West

ALTHOUGH Minnesota east of the Mississippi became American territory under the treaty of 1783, it was not until after the turn of the century that the first explorer to carry the Stars and Stripes entered the area. This was Zebulon M. Pike, who later discovered the Colorado mountain known as Pikes Peak. He was a young army lieutenant in 1805, when he traveled northward from St. Louis via the Mississippi. By that time Minnesota west of the great river had become American territory through the purchase from France of Louisiana—a vast empire which had been owned by Spain for forty years before it was transferred first to Napoleon and then to the United States for the sum of fifteen million dollars in 1803.

Among the objectives of Pike's journey was the selection of sites for military posts—forts that would provide protection for the fur traders and their lucrative wilderness business with the Indians. The explorer was instructed not only to purchase "from the Indians who claim the ground" land on which to build posts, but to bring about peace between the ever-warring tribes and to follow the Mississippi to its source. On an island in the Mississippi now known by his name, he held a council with the Sioux and obtained from them fort sites at the mouths of the St. Croix and Minnesota rivers. Although the Father of Waters had been known to white men for almost three centuries, the location of its headwaters remained a mystery—a mystery that Pike believed he had solved when he reached and added to the map Upper Red Cedar or Cass Lake on a frigid February day in 1806.

The same lake was again labeled the source of the great river in 1820 by an exploring party under Governor Lewis Cass of Michigan, whose name it still bears. Three years later Giacomo Constantino Beltrami searched independently for the Mississippi's headwaters. It remained, however, for Henry R. Schoolcraft to discover the stream's "true source" in 1832. He had gone with Cass as far as Cass Lake in 1820, but he did not agree with the governor's conclusion that this was the Mississippi's source. The In-

ZEBULON M. PIKE explored the Mississippi from St. Louis northward to Sandy, Leech, and Cass lakes in 1805–06, and he obtained from the Sioux the land on which Fort Snelling was built and still stands. *Courtesy National Archives, Washington, D.C.*

dians told him that a little river entering Cass Lake from the northwest flowed out of another lake. In order to ascend that stream to what he felt sure was the real beginning of the great river, Schoolcraft returned to the area after a lapse of twelve years. A Chippewa Indian, Ozawindib, or the Yellow Head, served as the explorer's guide as he pushed upstream to Lake Bemidji and then southwestward by way of the east fork of the Mississippi and a six-mile portage to the body of water known to the red men as Elk Lake. A hasty tour of the shore convinced the explorer that he had reached his long-sought goal.

Schoolcraft was prepared with a name—Itasca—coined from two Latin words recalled on the outward journey by a missionary in his party, the Reverend William T. Boutwell. After pausing briefly on Schoolcraft Island, the explorer followed the shore northward to the spot where the Mississippi leaves Lake Itasca as a "respectable stream" and then floated with the current to Cass Lake and Fort Snelling. There Schoolcraft announced that what Pike, Cass, and Beltrami had hoped to discover—the headwaters of the Mississippi—could be added to the map of the Minnesota country.

The findings of this persistent explorer were in time confirmed and mapped in great detail by two scientists. The first, Joseph N. Nicollet, a highly trained French astronomer and mathematician, traveled northward to Lake Itasca in the summer of

38

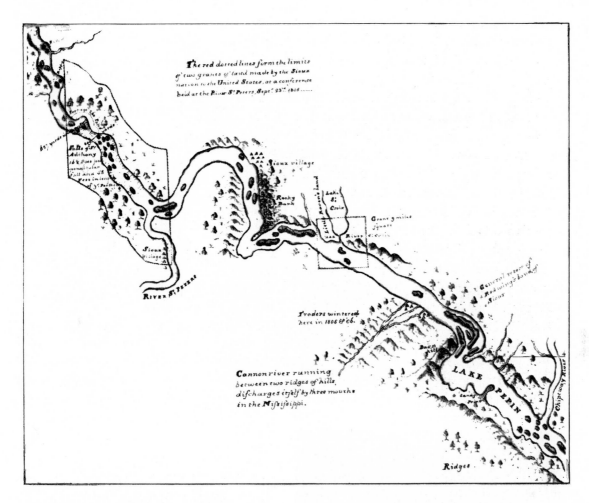

The red dotted lines form the limits of two grants of land made by the Sioux nation to the United States, at a conference held at the River St. Peters, Sept.r 23.d 1805.....

Sioux village

Rocky Bank

Lake St. Croix

Grant 9 miles square

River St. Croix

General resort of Red wing's band of Sioux

River St. Peters

Sioux village

Traders wintered here in 1805 & 06.

Cannon river running between two ridges of hills, discharges itself by three mouths in the Mississippi.

LAKE PEPIN

Chipeway River

Ridges

THE FORT SITES obtained by Pike are indicated on a huge manuscript map of the Mississippi Valley which Anthony Nau based on the explorer's notes. *Courtesy National Archives.*

A SKETCH OF THE MISSISIPPI

From the Town of St. Louis to its source in Upper Red Cedar Lake, exhibiting the communications with Lake Superior and the Lower Red River, a branch of the Ossiniboine River, of lake Winepie and marking the points at which the waters of the MISSISIPPI, the ST LAWRENCE and HUDSON'S BAY are separated. Taken from the notes of Lieutenant ZEBULON MONTGOMERY PIKE of the 1.st Reg.t of Infantry who traced the discovery made by him, pending the years 1805 and 1806, at the head of a Sergeant, Corporal and eighteen men.

By
Anthony Nau
Sworn Interpreter of the French Language,
TERRITORY OF LOUISIANA.

THE CARTOUCHE of Pike and Nau's map indicates that it marks the points "at which the waters of the Mississippi, the St. Lawrence and Hudson's Bay, are separated"—continental divides now within Minnesota's area. *Courtesy National Archives.*

1836, spending three full days in an examination of the locality which had detained Schoolcraft for only two hours. Since Nicollet carried with him the tools of his profession, he was equipped to determine the latitude, longitude, and height above sea level of the lake, and to carefully survey and map five tiny streamlets that feed it from the south. The largest, he decided, could be designated as "truly the infant Mississippi"; it was later named Nicollet Creek. This scientific explorer incorporated his findings about the Itasca area in a great map of the region stretching westward from the Mississippi to the Missouri which, in the words of William W. Folwell, "determined all the subsequent cartography of an immense region." More than four decades later, in 1888 and 1889, Jacob V. Brower made another careful topographic and hydrographic survey of the Itasca basin. Minnesotans are indebted to him for persuading the Minnesota legislature to establish Itasca State Park and to preserve in all its natural beauty the area where America's greatest river begins its long journey to the sea.

The Mississippi was not the only northern waterway that beckoned to explorers in the early nineteenth century. There was the Minnesota, then called the St. Peter's. Little was known about its course through the rolling prairie and Big Woods country to the west. The Red River also awaited investigation by trained map makers. Where did the international boundary cross this stream and where did that artificial line cut through the maze of lakes and rivers of the Canadian border area? Where were the best fort sites in the Minnesota country? What of the native tribes? Was the area

MAJOR STEPHEN H. LONG sat for this portrait in the spring of 1823 at Philadelphia while waiting for members of his Minnesota expedition to assemble. The original hangs in Independence Hall. *Oil by Charles Willson Peale, 1823; courtesy Eastern National Park and Monument Association, Philadelphia.*

BIG STONE LAKE, now on the western boundary of Minnesota, was pictured in this water color by Samuel Seymour, the artist who accompanied Long's expedition of 1823 and prepared the illustrations for William H. Keating's published narrative of the journey. *Courtesy Maryland Historical Society, Baltimore.*

suitable for white settlement? These were only a few of the questions waiting to be answered by government-organized expeditions and independent travelers.

Prominent among those who helped solve these problems was Major Stephen H. Long. He ascended the Mississippi from Prairie du Chien to the Falls of St. Anthony in a six-oared skiff in 1817, when he confirmed Pike's choice of a location for a military establishment at the mouth of the Minnesota. Six years later, after Fort Snelling had been built on the site, Long returned at the head of a military and scientific expedition. Its personnel included a geologist, a zoologist, an astronomer, and a landscape painter; the leader himself was a skilled cartographer. This party made a circuit of what became Minnesota, traveling by way of the Minnesota and Red rivers, marking the international boundary at the forty-ninth parallel, and following the border waters eastward to Lake Superior.

41

Others who carried the Stars and Stripes westward while exploring under government sponsorship included a long line of military men—Captain Matthew J. Magee, who made a trip in 1820, Stephen Watts Kearny, who was with Magee and who returned as a lieutenant colonel in charge of his own expedition in 1835, Lieutenant Albert Lea, Captain James Allen, Captain Edwin V. Sumner, Major Samuel Woods, Captain John Pope, Captain Jesse L. Reno, and Colonel Charles F. Smith. Most interesting of the independent travelers was George Catlin, an artist who went to Fort Snelling in the summers of 1835 and 1836, chiefly to sketch the Sioux. The reports of these adventurous pathfinders filled in many details on the map of Minnesota and carried the record of discovery in the area through the 1850s.

A new era of exploration began in 1853, when Isaac I. Stevens led an expedition westward from St. Paul to survey a northern route for a railroad to the Pacific. A West Point graduate who became governor of Washington Territory after reaching his goal on Puget Sound, Stevens not only mapped a trail for the iron horse from the upper Mississippi to the Western Sea, but he paved the way for Minnesota's future importance in the transportation history of the West.

GIACOMO CONSTANTINO BELTRAMI, an Italian adventurer, believed he had found the source of both the Mississippi and the Red rivers in Lake Julia, near Lower Red Lake. He published an account of his travels which is as romantic as this portrait "in his dress when among the Indians." *Frontispiece from Beltrami,* A Pilgrimage in Europe and America (*London, 1828*).

HENRY R. SCHOOLCRAFT discovered Lake Itasca and raised the Stars and Stripes on the island since known by his name on July 13, 1832. *Water color by Eastman, who based his picture on Schoolcraft's own sketch; courtesy Hill Reference Library.*

SCHOOLCRAFT'S MAP OF LAKE ITASCA shows his route from southeast to northwest. Four years after his journey, in August, 1836, the French scientist, Joseph N. Nicollet, added many details to this map. *From Schoolcraft, Narrative of an Expedition (New York, 1834).*

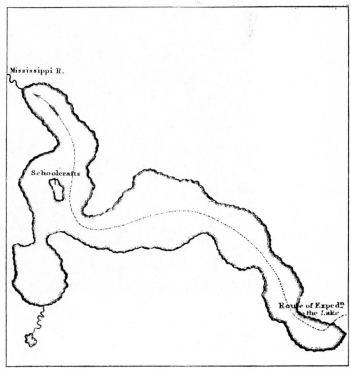

JOSEPH N. NICOLLET is pictured above at the American Fur Company's Crow Wing post while en route northward from Fort Snelling in 1836. Welcoming him is Allan Morrison, the trader in charge. *Mural by Sarah Thorp Heald in the Crow Wing County Courthouse, Brainerd.*

THE PIPESTONE QUARRY in southwestern Minnesota is Catlin's addition to the map of the state. He reached this sacred ground of the Indians in August, 1836, when he not only sketched it, but took away some specimens of the red stone, named "catlinite" in his honor. *Oil by Catlin, 1836; courtesy National Museum, Smithsonian Institution.*

6.

Civilization Marches North

AMERICAN SOLDIERS did not march into the upper Mississippi Valley to stay as representatives of the new United States until after the War of 1812. Some of these forerunners of civilization occupied the site of old British Fort McKay at Prairie du Chien and built a new base known as Fort Crawford in 1816. Three years later a group of military men arrived at the mouth of the Minnesota River to establish a still more remote island of civilized life in the wilderness—the post later named Fort Snelling.

John C. Calhoun, then secretary of war, planned the second fort to protect the fur trade and preserve peace in the Northland by keeping the Indians under control. To carry out his plans, Colonel Henry Leavenworth and about a hundred soldiers of the Fifth United States Infantry moved up the Mississippi in August, 1819, to the location originally selected by Pike in 1805 and confirmed by Long in 1817. With some recruits who arrived later, they spent a difficult winter in a crude camp known as New Hope near the present site of Mendota. With spring, Leavenworth moved his men to higher ground at Camp Coldwater, on the west bank of the Mississippi back of the later fort, where a natural spring provided an adequate supply of fresh water. As commandant, he was soon succeeded by Colonel Josiah Snelling, under whose supervision the permanent stone fort was built. It was originally called Fort St. Anthony, but after visiting the new post, General Winfield Scott recommended naming it "Fort Snelling" in honor of its builder. The name was changed officially in January, 1825.

The post thus established had a far-reaching influence on the development of the area that was destined to become the thirty-second state. For travelers and explorers, traders and missionaries, artists, authors, scientists, and any other hardy adventurers who might make their way so far north, Fort Snelling became a mecca in the wilderness, a symbol of civilization and hospitality and some degree of comfort on the remote frontier. During more than three decades this military installation served as the gateway to the country beyond.

COLONEL HENRY LEAVENWORTH established the military post that later became Fort Snelling. With him when he arrived in 1819 was Major Thomas Forsyth, an Indian agent, who distributed among the red men presents in payment for the land on which the fort was to be built.

Like the whites, the Indians looked upon Fort Snelling as a place of refuge, for at the post lived their agent, Major Lawrence Taliaferro. Upon arriving on the upper Mississippi in 1820, he promptly made his influence felt, and it soon became apparent that he put the red men's rights ahead of any demands made by traders or others interested in exploiting the natives. Taliaferro's truthfulness in dealing with his charges and his tolerance for their love of ceremony inspired their lasting confidence. He served as agent for both the Sioux and the Chippewa until 1827, when the latter's agency was transferred to Mackinac. His many duties included keeping peace between the warring tribes, settling disputes between Indians and traders, issuing licenses to traders, attending Indian treaties, holding councils with the natives, paying annuities, receiving all red men who chanced to visit Fort Snelling, and encouraging agriculture and education among the Indians.

In implementing the civilizing features of his program, Taliaferro found the services of the Protestant missionaries especially valuable. When two brothers from Connecticut, Samuel and Gideon Pond, appeared at Fort Snelling bent on converting and educating the Sioux, the agent gave them every encouragement and helped them

CANTONMENT NEW HOPE was the winter home of the men who traveled upstream with Colonel Leavenworth in 1819. Because the location proved unhealthful, the colonel moved his men to higher ground in the spring of 1820. *Pencil drawing, evidently based on descriptions, by Ada B. Morvill.*

establish schools and cultivate farms for the Indians in neighboring villages. The Reverend Stephen R. Riggs and Dr. Thomas S. Williamson were among other missionaries who looked to Taliaferro for support in their work among the red men in an area extending westward from Little Crow's village near present-day South St. Paul to Lac qui Parle in the upper Minnesota Valley.

Because Fort Snelling was never the scene of active conflict, its history is unique in the annals of the frontier. The soldiers stationed there played the role of protectors first for traders and later for pioneer settlers who worked in safety with ax and plow in the comforting shadow of its walls.

This peaceful installation remained the only military post in Minnesota and the northernmost fort on the upper Mississippi until 1849. Then the movement of settlers northward and the transfer of the Winnebago Indians from Iowa to a reservation near Long Prairie provided the incentive for establishing Fort Ripley near the present city

ABIGAIL HUNT SNELLING accompanied her soldier husband to Fort Snelling, where she played a significant role as a woman of culture in a frontier environment and as a pioneer hostess and homemaker. The Snelling portraits are oils, probably painted about 1825.

of Little Falls. The need for military protection by newcomers who moved into the Minnesota Valley after the treaties of 1851 were ratified was met in 1853 by the building of Fort Ridgely. Another post, Fort Abercrombie, intended to protect settlers in the Red River Valley, was established in 1858 on the west bank of that stream within Minnesota Territory but just beyond the border of the new state. Soldiers from Fort Snelling, especially members of the picturesque First Dragoons long stationed there, were instrumental in the founding of these three posts, all of which were to play significant roles in the great Indian war of the 1860s.

With the westward movement of settlers, the removal of the Indians from eastern Minnesota, and the building of Forts Ripley, Ridgely, and Abercrombie in mid-century, Fort Snelling lost much of its importance in Minnesota and the Northwest. In 1858 troops were actually withdrawn, but with the outbreak of the Civil War the fort again came into use as a training center. It was the only Minnesota post to continue in military service through the Spanish-American and the First and Second World wars, functioning in the nation's defense until October, 1946.

48

COLONEL JOSIAH SNELLING, for whom the fort is named, succeeded Leavenworth as commandant, serving from August, 1820, to January, 1828. He not only planned the permanent stone fortification, but he chose the exact location for the post and supervised its erection.

FORT SNELLING began with the laying of its cornerstone on September 10, 1820, and the wall and principal buildings were completed in 1823. They were constructed largely of local limestone quarried by the soldiers. To meet the need for lumber, these frontier military men cut pine logs on the Rum River and rafted them downstream to the Falls of St. Anthony, where they built the first sawmill to harness its power. *Drawing by Dr. Nathan S. Jarvis, 1833.*

FORT SNELLING, with its dramatic location on the heights overlooking both the Minnesota and the Mississippi, drew the attention of every traveler and artist who visited the vicinity. The view at the right, from Mendota across the Minnesota River, shows the Sibley House in the foreground and the buildings of the Indian agency at the rear of the fort. Among the latter were the agent's residence, a council house, and a blacksmith shop. The boat approaching the landing suggests the river traffic that began in 1823 with the arrival of the "Virginia," the first steamboat to navigate the upper Mississippi. *Gouache and pastel by J. C. Wild, 1844.*

THE INTERIOR of Fort Snelling (below), which is rarely pictured, is the subject of this little water color by George F. Fuller, a civil engineer who helped make a topographical survey of the fort area in 1853. The buildings at the left housed offices and the post church; the powder magazine is depicted in front of the Round Tower; and at the right is the well with a section of the enclosing wall behind it.

THE WALLS of Fort Snelling outlined a diamond-shaped enclosure, with the commandant's house and a lookout tower at the point above the junction of the two rivers. Opposite was the Round Tower, from the top of which Adolf Hoeffler sketched this view in 1852. Clearly depicted are the Hexagonal Tower overlooking the Minnesota on the right, and the Pentagonal Tower above the Mississippi on the left. *Engraving based on Hoeffler's sketch, in* Harper's New Monthly Magazine, *July, 1853.*

A FERRY across the Mississippi provided communication between Fort Snelling and St. Paul before 1880, when the first bridge to connect them was built. *Photograph by B. F. Upton, 1867.*

THE FIRST UNITED STATES DRAGOONS were closely identified with Fort Snelling from the organization of the regiment in 1833. On various occasions, the dragoons marched into the country west and north of Fort Snelling, exploring it and selecting sites for other military posts. The dragoon here pictured in dress uniform was sketched by Mayer at Fort Snelling in 1851. *Courtesy New York Public Library.*

THE THIRD UNITED STATES ARTILLERY, also known as Sherman's Battery, was stationed at Fort Snelling much of the time from 1853 to 1857, when its chief officer, Major Thomas W. Sherman, was commandant of the post. The battery is shown above in October, 1855, drilling on the open prairie that stretched westward behind the fort. Three of the fortification's four towers and the connecting walls may be seen in this view. *Water color by Alfred Sully; courtesy Gilcrease Institute of American History and Art.*

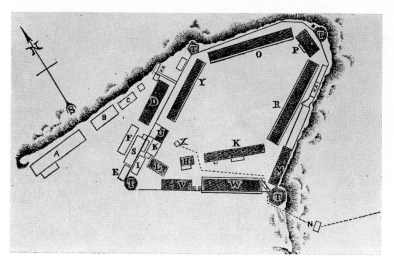

STONE BUILDINGS are represented by shading in this diagram of Fort Snelling. All except that marked "D" were erected before the Civil War. *From the Surgeon General's* Report on Barracks and Hospitals *(Washington, 1870).*

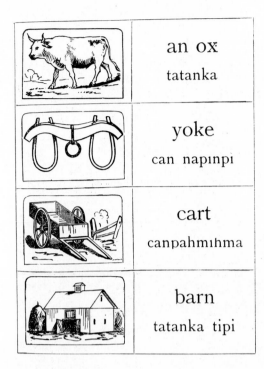

	an ox tatanka
	yoke can napınpı
	cart canpahmıhma
	barn tatanka tipi

ENGLISH-DAKOTA BOOKS used in the mission schools included Stephen R. Riggs' *Model First Reader: Wayawa Tokaheya* (Chicago, 1875), from which this illustration is reproduced. With Taliaferro's encouragement, schools for Indian children were established on Lake Harriet in 1835 by a missionary named Jedediah Stevens. While working with him there, the Pond brothers began a study of the Dakota language which eventually resulted in the publication of a *Grammar and Dictionary of the Dakota Language*, edited by Riggs (Washington, 1852).

CLOUDMAN'S VILLAGE on Lake Calhoun was the scene of one of Major Taliaferro's experiments in civilizing the Indians. On the shore of this lovely lake, within the present limits of Minneapolis, he persuaded a few Sioux families to establish an agricultural colony. The Pond brothers began their long careers as Protestant missionaries to the Sioux at Lake Calhoun. *Oil by Catlin, about 1835; courtesy National Museum, Smithsonian Institution.*

54

MAJOR LAWRENCE TALIAFERRO, Indian agent at Fort Snelling from 1820 to 1840, was appointed by President Monroe in 1819 to conduct Indian affairs at the new post. The walls of the fort, the agency house, and a group of red men appear in the background of this oil portrait by an unknown artist, suggesting that it was painted during Taliaferro's term as agent.

FORT RIPLEY, originally called Fort Gaines, was built on the upper Mississippi near Little Falls by dragoons and infantrymen from Fort Snelling in 1848–49. The new post, which replaced Fort Snelling as the northernmost military installation on the Mississippi, was intended to control the Chippewa and the Winnebago, who occupied a reservation between Chippewa and Sioux territory for a few years after 1848. *Wash drawing by August Harfeldt, 1862.*

CROSS SECTION of a blockhouse at Fort Ripley. *From a manuscript plan of the post, 1864.*

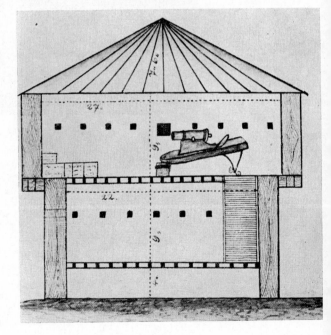

FORT ABERCROMBIE was located on the Red River, in the heart of Minnesota's third great valley, in the autumn of 1857. The site, on the stream's west bank about twenty miles north of the mouth of the Bois des Sioux, was in Minnesota Territory when the fort was built by Colonel John J. Abercrombie, for whom it was named. After Minnesota became a state in 1858, the new post was outside its western boundary in what became Dakota Territory. *Wash drawing by Sweeny, 1862.*

FORT RIDGELY, on the Minnesota River above New Ulm, was established in 1853. Founded to protect settlers and to control the Sioux, who were transferred to a Minnesota Valley reservation in the summer of 1853, the fort played a major role in the Sioux Outbreak of 1862. *Water color by Sully, 1855; courtesy Gilcrease Institute of American History and Art.*

7.

Vanguard of Settlement

FORT SNELLING was the nucleus about which the earliest Minnesota settlements evolved. Strangely enough, the homeseekers who constituted the state's vanguard of settlement migrated to the fort's vicinity not from the east or the south, but from the north. They came as refugees from the Red River country beyond the Canadian border—from the colony of Assiniboia founded by the altruistic Earl of Selkirk in 1811. To lands granted by the Hudson's Bay Company, he and his agents lured Scotch, Irish, Swiss, and German peasants, promising them farms in a peaceful and fruitful district. These unfortunate people, however, soon became involved in open warfare between the Hudson's Bay and North West companies, and such crops as they were able to raise were destroyed by floods, grasshoppers, or drouth. The calamities they were forced to face and the severity of the winters caused them to leave in large numbers, many going to the first outpost of civilization beyond the border—Fort Snelling. On a single June day in 1826, a total of 243 colonists headed south from Pembina. All went to the Minnesota post, and many remained to cultivate farms as squatters on the military reservation. Among those who followed the future route of the Red River cart trains southward were members of a Swiss family named Rindisbacher, one of whom, Peter, was a skilled artist. Some of his vivid pictorial records of people and places in the Red River colony are reproduced in this chapter.

Although many of the emigrants pushed on to areas farther south, eventually settling in the French communities along the Mississippi in Illinois and Missouri, it seems likely that the greater proportion established homes near Fort Snelling. A census taken by an army officer from the post in 1837 revealed that "a total of 157 souls in no way connected with the military" were living in the vicinity. Two years later the Catholic bishop of Dubuque, Mathias Loras, paid a visit to the area and counted 185 members of his church in the neighborhood. Doubtless included in these figures were a number of French-Canadian traders and voyageurs who, with their families, had established

58

themselves on the west bank of the Minnesota at Mendota, the headquarters of the American Fur Company for the entire upper Mississippi and the valley drained by its tributaries.

Since no part of the present state of Minnesota was open to settlement until 1838, most of the people living near Fort Snelling were of necessity squatters, illegally occupying the lands on which they lived. The reservation, obtained from the Indians for military purposes, was the only white man's ground in the area. Two treaties of 1837 radically changed the situation. The first was negotiated at Fort Snelling with the Chippewa, and the second at Washington with the Sioux. Under their terms, the Indians ceded all lands between the St. Croix and the Mississippi in return for annuities and other grants. When the treaties were ratified by the Senate in June, 1838, a triangular section of eastern Minnesota became the first portion of the future state legally available to settlers.

From the Fort Snelling area, where many of them had been quietly living and farming for more than a decade, the Red River people were ordered to move into the region which was open to settlement. They selected lands across the Mississippi opposite the post—lands they firmly believed were outside the military reservation. A survey, how-

FORT GARRY, known earlier as Fort Douglas, is visible in the center background of this view painted by one of the settlers in 1822. The post was situated in the northern Red River area, from which people of varied origins migrated southward to Fort Snelling after Selkirk's colony met with disaster. *Water color by Rindisbacher, 1822; courtesy Public Archives of Canada.*

RED RIVER COLONISTS, pictured above in a settler's house, include, from left to right, a Swiss housewife, a Scotch Highlander, the Swiss householder and his children, a German, and a French Canadian. Members of these groups crossed the border in the 1820s and became Minnesota's earliest settlers. *Sketch by Rindisbacher, about 1824; courtesy Public Archives of Canada.*

ever, showed that they were still living within its limits, which extended beyond the river's east bank, and in May, 1840, after being forcibly evicted, they moved farther eastward onto ground that later became the center of St. Paul's first business district. The new settlers' claims were near that staked a year earlier by a Canadian voyageur who engaged in selling whisky to the soldiers—one Pierre Parrant, better known as "Pig's Eye." To this unsavory character goes the credit for being the first settler on the site of the future Minnesota capital. The little settlement was even called "Pig's Eye" until the autumn of 1841, when Father Lucian Galtier built a crude log church for the French-speaking Catholics in the new community on the Mississippi. The pioneer priest dedicated his chapel "to St. Paul, the apostle of nations," and from it the embryo city took a permanent name.

By the late 1840s, the original French-speaking group at St. Paul had been joined by numerous Yankees and other ambitious American pioneers; a post office had been es-

MENDOTA, the chief post for the American Fur Company's Sioux Outfit, was a center of settlement for its traders and other employees, white and mixed-blood, who worked in and about buildings like this. There were stored furs collected as far north as Pembina and as far west as the Missouri, in addition to trade goods carried up the Mississippi on steamboats. Henry H. Sibley, a youthful agent and partner of the American Fur Company, arrived to take charge of the Mendota trade in October, 1834. *Photograph taken in the 1860s.*

tablished; a regular line of steamboats connected the new settlement with older communities down the Mississippi; and a flourishing trade, conducted largely in ox-drawn carts, had developed with the Canadian Red River country. The vanguard of settlement also began to penetrate the St. Croix Valley, where logging operations were quickly followed by the building of sawmills at Marine, Stillwater, and other communities. A third center of population evolved on the east bank of the Mississippi at the Falls of St. Anthony, where early and grist saw mills served as harbingers of vast industrial plants to come. As soon as the treaties of 1837 were ratified, claims were promptly staked there by Franklin Steele, a pioneer who well appreciated the commercial possibilities of the site. At the first public land sale in the area, held at St. Croix Falls in 1848, the onetime squatters at St. Paul and the claimants of other choice localities paid for their lands at the rate of $1.25 an acre and became legal owners. Thus began settlement in the future state of Minnesota.

61

THE SIBLEY HOUSE, a substantial residence built by the trader at Mendota in 1835, contrasts sharply with the structures in which his many employees worked and lived. In his home, where he surrounded himself with such evidences of culture as a piano and an extensive library, Sibley entertained visitors to the upper river. The house, which is still standing, is now the oldest residence in the state and is maintained as a museum by the Minnesota Daughters of the American Revolution. *Water color by Mrs. John M. Armstrong, painted about 1888.*

SARAH STEELE SIBLEY met her frontiersman husband in Baltimore, when he attended the wedding of her brother, Franklin Steele. From the day of their marriage at Fort Snelling in 1843 until the couple moved to St. Paul in 1862, she served as hostess in the handsome stone house at Mendota.

FATHER LUCIAN GALTIER left his native France in 1838 to become a Catholic missionary in the wilds of western America. After Bishop Loras visited the Mendota area in 1839 and found numerous Catholics living in the vicinity without the services of a priest, he sent Father Galtier there in the spring of 1840 to minister to these isolated pioneers.

A LOG CHAPEL built at Mendota by Father Galtier marked the beginning of that community's St. Peter's Church. It was attended largely by French-speaking traders and voyageurs employed by the fur company. The original log structure was used as a public school for more than a decade after 1853, when a stone church was erected. *Sketch by C. M. Crowley, based on reminiscent descriptions, 1917; courtesy St. Paul Seminary.*

THE CHAPEL OF ST. PAUL was built by Father Galtier near the grogshop of "Pig's Eye" Parrant in October, 1841, and dedicated on November 1. The settlement soon took the name of the log chapel, becoming known as St. Paul's Landing or St. Paul's, and finally simply as St. Paul. *Oil by Sweeny, 1852.*

THE SETTLERS served by the Chapel of St. Paul included Pierre Bottineau and Vital Guerin. Bottineau (left), a half-breed from Red River, went to Fort Snelling in 1837 and was among the squatters evicted from the reservation. He became a famous scout, acting as guide and interpreter for many a western exploring and hunting expedition. Guerin, who was a voyageur for the American Fur Company at Mendota as early 1832, built a cabin in 1839 in what later became the heart of St. Paul. The photograph reproduced below was taken by Joel E. Whitney. Among other pioneer settlers on the site of the future city were Abraham Perry, Benjamin and Pierre Gervais, and Joseph Rondo. By 1845 there were some thirty families in the little settlement, most of them of French and Canadian origin.

ST. PAUL in 1848 consisted of trading houses near the river at the foot of Jackson Street and cabins and houses on higher ground built by pioneers from Canada, New England, and other points east and south. The lands on which they had established homes were offered for sale at the St. Croix Falls land office in the summer of 1848. After having some ninety acres surveyed and platted, the St. Paulites attended the sale in a body, accompanied by their friend and neighbor Henry H. Sibley, who did the bidding for all. By acquiring deeds for their lands, the former squatters on the site of the future capital became property owners and settlers. *Lithograph in Henry Lewis,* Das illustrirte Mississippithal *(Düsseldorf, 1858).*

THE TRADING STORE of William H. Forbes at Third and Robert streets, St. Paul, housed the local "outfit" of the American Fur Company from 1847 until 1853, when the firm closed its business in the Minnesota capital. Forbes continued to trade with the Indians as a partner of N. W. Kittson. *Sketch by Sweeny, 1852.*

THE FIRST ST. PAUL POST OFFICE (right) was merely a crude box divided into pigeon holes, constructed by Henry Jackson, who became the city's pioneer postmaster in 1846. Business grew so rapidly that it soon required the separate building pictured at the left in Sweeny's sketch of 1852. It was located on Third Street below Minnesota. The box is now in the museum collection of the Minnesota Historical Society.

A LOG HOUSE built at what became Snelling and St. Anthony avenues in St. Paul by Lot Moffet, a New Yorker who moved west in 1848, was later acquired by Auguste L. Larpenteur, a settler of 1843 from Baltimore. They were among the numerous Easterners who established homes in the future capital in the 1840s. *Pen-and-ink drawing by J. Desuarreaux Larpenteur.*

ELAM GREELEY was one of the numerous New Englanders who settled at Stillwater in the 1840s. With John McKusick he built a sawmill there in the spring of 1844, and in 1845 he became the community's first postmaster. Other Yankee pioneers living there were Anson Northup, who built the first public house, and Socrates Nelson, who opened the first store. Stillwater became the second center of settlement in preterritorial Minnesota. It was peopled largely by lumbermen from Maine and other New England states, and it developed as a logging center.

MARINE MILLS grew up about the first sawmill in the St. Croix Valley, included at the extreme left of this picture. Among the enterprising pioneers who rushed into the valley after the treaties of 1837 were ratified were Lewis S. Judd and David Hone, representatives of a lumber company at Marine, Illinois. They selected the site of the future town and, with other colonists from Illinois, built the mill in 1839. The concern eventually became Walker, Judd and Veazie. *Woodcut by Peter Hugenine, about 1880; courtesy Charles J. Brown, Marine.*

A MILL AT ST. CROIX FALLS, known in 1848 as Cheever's Mill, utilized water power that was first exploited by a company organized at St. Louis in 1838. Two years later some of its members staked a claim on the east bank of the river and built a sawmill opposite what is now Taylors Falls. *Oil by Henry Lewis, based on a sketch of 1848; courtesy Minneapolis Institute of Arts.*

67

MILLS were built by the federal government on the west bank of the river at the Falls of St. Anthony long before the days of settlement. The water power of the cataract was first exploited in 1821, when soldiers erected the sawmill at the extreme right of this picture to produce lumber for the building of Fort Snelling. Two years later they built the grist mill shown in the center. These mills, used by the military personnel stationed at the fort, foreshadowed the future commercial development which gave rise to Minnesota's largest city. *Photograph by Upton, 1857.*

THE FALLS OF ST. ANTHONY, here pictured in their original beauty, provided a potentially profitable location for a settlement as soon as the treaties of 1837 opened the east bank of the Mississippi to land-seekers. *Oil by Henry Lewis, 1848.*

FRANKLIN STEELE seems to have been the first of the eager pioneers who rushed to the Falls of St. Anthony to stake claims. He supposedly had a cabin near the water-power site as early as 1838. By 1845 he had obtained all the land in the vicinity; in 1847 he built a dam across the east channel of the river; and a year later he had a sawmill in operation on the east bank.

THE VILLAGE OF ST. ANTHONY FALLS developed as lumbermen began to move into the area from Stillwater and St. Paul, as well as from the East and South. Laborers, tradesmen, and professional people followed in rapid succession. In 1849 a town plat for the new community was prepared by a future Minnesota governor, William R. Marshall. By 1850, a third substantial settlement had evolved in the Minnesota triangle—a settlement whose pioneer residents heard in the roar of the cataract a song of future prosperity. *Daguerreotype taken about 1855.*

TIMBER in plentiful supply stimulated the early development of water power at the Falls of St. Anthony. This view, taken from the east bank of the Mississippi, shows logs floated from pineries situated upstream, probably on the Rum River. *Daguerreotype taken about 1851.*

8.

Minnesota Becomes
a Territory

THE MINNESOTA COUNTRY, with its three embryo communities of St. Paul, St. Anthony, and Stillwater, faced a major crisis in 1848. The river-bordered triangle between the Mississippi and the St. Croix had been part of Wisconsin Territory ever since 1836; earlier it had been attached successively to the Northwest Territory and the territories of Indiana, Illinois, and Michigan. Some of its residents, notably Joseph R. Brown, had participated actively in Wisconsin's territorial affairs. Then on May 29, 1848, Wisconsin was admitted to the Union as a state bounded on the west by the St. Croix. Beyond was the rump of the onetime territory—a district that, in the words of a Minnesota historian, became "a no-man's land without law or government." After long enjoying the benefits of territorial rule under rapidly changing auspices, the people living on this neglected frontier found themselves "without corporate existence."

Out of this situation developed a demand for the organization of a territory to be called Minnesota. Agitation centered at Stillwater, just outside the limits of the new state of Wisconsin, where a public meeting was followed by a "convention" on August 26, 1848. The sixty-one delegates who assembled at Stillwater that day drafted memorials to Congress and to the president calling for the "early organization of the Territory of Minnesota." In a somewhat unconventional election held in October, Henry H. Sibley was chosen to represent the rump of Wisconsin Territory in Washington and to work for the interests of the proposed territory of Minnesota.

When Congress convened on December 4, Sibley was on hand to present his certificate of election, and in due course it was somewhat surprisingly approved by the appropriate committee. With substantial help from Senator Stephen A. Douglas and others, the delegate obtained the passage, on March 3, 1849, of a bill creating Minnesota Territory. Some five weeks later, on April 9, the first steamboat of the season drew up to the St. Paul levee, bringing with it the heartening news that the measure had been passed.

70

STILLWATER was the scene of the convention of 1848 which constituted the first step toward territorial organization. Two of the buildings in this view—the Minnesota House at the right and the St. Croix House at the extreme left—were built before the convention assembled. *Photograph taken in 1870.*

The new commonwealth embraced a huge area extending westward to the Missouri. Politically, the section between that river and the Mississippi had a background completely different from the district east of the Father of Waters. Much of the former region was included in the Louisiana Purchase, and in turn it had been part of the territories of Louisiana, Missouri, Michigan, Wisconsin, and Iowa. After Iowa attained statehood in 1846, the area beyond its northern border was left without organized government. But unlike the St. Croix-Mississippi triangle, western Minnesota was not open to settlement, and with few exceptions its widely scattered residents had little influence on the organization of the territory. One all-important exception, of course, was Sibley, who lived west of the Mississippi at Mendota.

Only two days after Minnesota became a territory, President Zachary Taylor took office, and he named its first officials. His original choice for the governorship, which was considered "one of the two or three most desirable domestic noncabinet positions"

71

he was privileged to fill, was Edward W. McGaughey of Indiana. The Senate, however, for purely political reasons, rejected him. Taylor then chose William Pennington of New Jersey, but he declined the office. The name of Alexander Ramsey, which was destined to loom large in the annals of Minnesota, was the third submitted by the president. This active Whig from Pennsylvania, who had represented his state in Congress for two terms, became Minnesota's first territorial governor. Other appointees included Aaron Goodrich, chief justice; David Cooper and Bradley B. Meeker, judges of the supreme court; Alexander M. Mitchell, marshal; Henry L. Moss, district attorney; and Charles K. Smith, secretary. To the new territorial capital of St. Paul these men traveled in the spring of 1849. On June 1 Ramsey declared the territorial government established.

A proclamation issued by the new governor early in July divided the territory into legislative districts and ordered the election of nine councilors, as members of the upper house were called, eighteen representatives, and a delegate to represent Minnesota in the national House of Representatives in Washington. In the election which followed on August 1, Sibley was named to succeed himself as Congressional delegate. The first legislature convened in St. Paul on September 3. As secretary of the council, Joe Brown capitalized on his earlier experience in the Wisconsin territorial assembly. Brown was only one of the colorful frontiersmen who served in Minnesota's territorial legislature. Among others were Norman W. Kittson and Joe Rolette, fur traders from Pembina on the west bank of the Red River near the Canadian boundary, who traveled the more than four hundred miles to St. Paul on snowshoes or by dog sled in order to attend the midwinter legislative sessions.

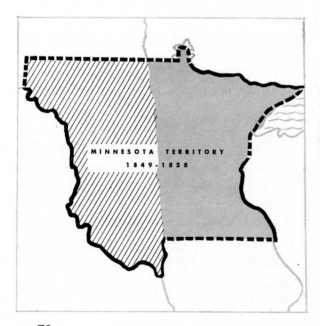

MINNESOTA TERRITORY, bounded on the west by the Missouri and White Earth rivers, embraced much of the area now occupied by the states of North and South Dakota.

JOSEPH R. BROWN, a leader in the Stillwater convention, had a long and varied experience in pioneering. He arrived at the future Fort Snelling in 1819 as a drummer boy of fourteen; he traded and cut logs on the St. Croix as early as 1837; he served in the Wisconsin territorial assembly from 1840 to 1842; and he established a townsite, known as Dakotah, which became a part of Stillwater. *Photograph by J. Byerly, 1858.*

HENRY H. SIBLEY worked for the organization of Minnesota Territory in Congress following the Stillwater convention, surprising the nation's lawmakers with his dapper appearance, stately bearing, polished manners, and familiarity with parliamentary procedure. Altogether, he made a favorable impression that did much to speed through Congress the bill for the organization of Minnesota Territory. *Photograph in the Sibley House, Mendota; courtesy Sibley House Association of the Minnesota Daughters of the American Revolution.*

ALEXANDER RAMSEY was a vigorous young man of thirty-three when he accepted the governorship of the new Territory of Minnesota in 1849. In Pennsylvania he had served as chairman of the Whig central committee during the election campaign of 1848, and the gubernatorial appointment was his reward for his party's decisive victory in his home state. He became an ardent Minnesotan, playing a leading role in the development of his adopted home for more than half a century. *Daguerreotype, about 1844; courtesy Misses Anna E. R. and Laura Furness, St. Paul.*

RAMSEY'S FIRST RESIDENCE in St. Paul was a house on Third Street between Robert and Jackson. He arrived with his wife, his three-year-old son, and a nurse on May 27, 1849, after a journey by steamboat, rail, and stage which involved a total outlay of $262.25. The house, which was being remodeled, was not yet ready, and the Ramseys spent their first month in Minnesota at Mendota as guests of the Sibleys. *Sketch by Sweeny, 1852.*

An act to "establish and maintain common schools" was perhaps the most important passed by the first legislature. Its author, Martin McLeod, was a fur trader who migrated southward from the Red River Settlement in 1837. Under the provisions of a law passed on October 20, 1849, the Minnesota Historical Society, the territory's first cultural institution, was chartered.

Cultural leanings were noticeable, too, in the second legislative session, which in 1851 passed a bill to incorporate the University of Minnesota. It was agreed that this institution of higher learning should be situated at St. Anthony. A spirited contest developed before the legislators approved a bill locating the territorial capitol at St. Paul and the prison at Stillwater. Such favors as the territorial legislature could bestow were thus divided among the three preterritorial population centers concentrated east of the Mississippi.

The housing of government offices, the prison, and the university in buildings of their own encountered many delays. The two houses of the territorial legislature met in joint session to listen to Governor Ramsey's annual messages in such varied places as the Baptist Church of St. Paul and the Ramsey County Courthouse, erected in 1851 to accommodate local officials and courts. The legislature held its first session in a St. Paul hotel, and as late as 1853 it assembled in a rented structure at Third and Minnesota streets. Minnesota's first Capitol finally was erected in the latter year, and it was ready for occupancy when members of the fifth legislature gathered for the session of 1854.

MARTIN McLEOD, a fur trader from Lac qui Parle who represented his district in the first territorial council, drafted Minnesota's first law establishing common schools. *Sketch by Mayer, 1851; courtesy Newberry Library, Chicago.*

USING DOG SLEDS like that pictured above, legislators from Pembina traveled to St. Paul for some sessions of the territorial legislature. When they reached the capital in the winter of 1852, "each had his cariole, drawn by three fine dogs, harnessed tastily, with jingling bells, and driven tandem fashion." *Photograph taken on the streets of St. Paul, 1857.*

The prison at Stillwater materialized about the same time; the building was first used in 1853, when the earliest warden took office. Less pressing, no doubt, was the need for a university building. Although the institution opened a preparatory department at St. Anthony with a single professor and twenty pupils as early as November, 1851, seven years passed before its first building was erected on the present Minneapolis campus.

By the time the Minnesota Capitol was occupied, Ramsey was no longer governor. With other Whig appointees of President Taylor, he was replaced when a Democratic administration came into power in 1853. The new president, Franklin Pierce, named Willis A. Gorman, a congressman from Indiana with a distinguished military record, to the governorship. Like his predecessor, Gorman served four years as territorial governor, and like Ramsey he continued to make Minnesota his home after a Democratic president, in this case James Buchanan, deprived him of his office. In April, 1857, Minnesota's third territorial governor, Samuel Medary of Ohio, arrived in St. Paul. He remained little more than a year; upon Minnesota's admission to the Union in May, 1858, he left the new state to become governor of Kansas Territory. Thus three men and two political parties controlled Minnesota's destinies through its nine-year territorial era. When the third took office, Minnesotans were already dreaming of statehood.

THE CENTRAL HOUSE, a St. Paul hotel at Bench and Minnesota Streets, attained distinction as Minnesota's first territorial capitol when the legislative assembly convened there on September 3, 1849. Members of the council and the house of representatives met in joint session in the dining room on the following day to listen to the governor's message. *Sketch by Sweeny, 1852.*

76

THE RAMSEY COUNTY COURTHOUSE made space available for a joint session of the legislature on January 26, 1853, when Ramsey delivered his final message as territorial governor. The building, erected in the winter of 1850–51 at Fourth and Wabasha streets, was planned by Dr. David Day, who received ten dollars for his design. *Photograph by Upton.*

THE PRISON AT STILLWATER began with two buildings erected in 1852–53. With many later additions, it remained in use until 1914, two years after the present institution was opened. *Photograph probably taken in the 1860s.*

THE FIRST BUILDING on the campus of the University of Minnesota, erected in 1858, became the west wing of "Old Main," which continued to provide space for classrooms until the entire structure was destroyed by fire shortly after the turn of the century. *Photograph taken in 1885.*

77

9.

Buying an Empire

THE IMPORTANCE of purchasing from the Sioux their vast empire west of the Mississippi was stressed by Governor Ramsey in his first message to the territorial legislature. "Once thrown open for settlement," the governor predicted, this "extensive, rich and salubrious region . . . would be peopled with a rapidity exceeding anything in the history of western civilization." The speed with which emigrants poured into the territory after its organization gave validity to this prediction and emphasized the need for lands upon which newcomers could settle. Promptly, the legislature followed the governor's suggestion that it "memorialize Congress upon the subject" of a treaty with the Sioux.

Although steps looking toward the purchase of what was popularly known as the "Suland" were taken earlier in Washington, it was not until the summer of 1851 that final arrangements for a treaty of cession were completed. After Governor Ramsey, who served as superintendent of Indian affairs in the territory, and Luke Lea, United States commissioner of Indian affairs, were named treaty commissioners, it was agreed to hold separate councils with the Upper and the Lower Sioux. At Traverse des Sioux in July and at Mendota in August, the commissioners met with the red men. Their negotiations at each place reached a dramatic climax in the signing of a treaty.

In response to a call carried by runners to the chiefs and headmen of the Plains tribes, a motley and colorful horde gathered at Traverse des Sioux in the early days of July, 1851. There were Indians of the Sisseton and Wahpeton bands decked out in full regalia, half-breeds looking for favors, fur traders and voyageurs from posts throughout the Northwest, government officials and clerks connected with the Indian office in Washington, Indian agents, journalists, missionaries, and others who were drawn to the scene by hope of personal gain or by mere curiosity. Among them was a Baltimore artist, Frank B. Mayer, whose sketches and water colors provide a pictorial record of the treaty story.

78

SISSETON SIOUX from the Lake Traverse area arrived at Traverse des Sioux in large numbers on July 4. With them they brought their wives, children, dogs, horses, and lodges. These horsemen of the Plains were great buffalo hunters, and they were as yet largely uncontaminated by white civilization. *Water color by Mayer, 1899; courtesy Goucher College.*

The commissioners and their official party, a group of traders headed by Henry H. Sibley, and numerous others left Fort Snelling for Traverse des Sioux on the steamboat "Excelsior" on June 29. Upon reaching the treaty grounds, they found only a few Indians, but the western tribesmen, including large groups of Sisseton from Lake Traverse and Wahpeton from Lac qui Parle, soon began to arrive. On the prairie, high above the beautiful Minnesota Valley, whites and Indians alike encamped, the former living in tents and the latter in tipis. In the weeks that followed both groups enjoyed a glorified camping party. The Indians feasted on pork, beef, flour, and other government rations, and entertained their hosts with games, dances, and similar ceremonies. The commissioners, traders, and other white men ate their meals in an abandoned trader's cabin. They seem to have spent much time visiting, reading, watching the Indians, listening to the voyageurs sing their traditional ballads, or simply reclining in their tents. On one occasion the visiting treaty makers were guests at the wedding of two half-breeds, Nancy McClure and David Faribault. Alexis Bailly performed the ceremony, reading the Episcopal service. At the gay dinner party which followed, congratulations and toasts were punctuated by popping corks, as champagne flowed freely throughout the celebration.

THE BUFFALO DANCE, which was designed to induce the bison to appear and furnish food, was performed by the Sisseton at the Traverse for the first time on July 17, with only a few dancers participating, and again by a much larger number on July 24. The dancers wore buffalo masks over their heads and shoulders and carried shields, spears, guns, and fans. After performing, they expected the white visitors to give them presents. *Water color by Mayer, about 1898; courtesy Goucher College.*

THE MANDAN DANCE, performed by some of the Sisseton assembled at the Traverse, centered about a highly ornamented drum on which the dancers beat in turn and sometimes in unison. Each performer described some of his exploits at one point in the dance, and concluded by begging and receiving a gift of tobacco. *Water color by Mayer, about 1898; courtesy Goucher College.*

80

Finally, on July 18, a sufficient number of Indians had assembled and the council began. The negotiations were conducted under a canopy of green boughs over a framework of young trees, and there, too, the treaty was signed on July 23. By its terms the Sisseton and Wahpeton Indians agreed to sell to the United States some thirty-five million acres of land in southern Minnesota, Iowa, and Dakota—an undeveloped empire stretching from the Mississippi, the Minnesota, and the Blue Earth rivers on the east to the Bois des Sioux and Big Sioux rivers on the west. For this wide domain, including some of the richest agricultural lands in Minnesota and Iowa, the government agreed to pay the Indians $1,665,000. The red men reserved for their own use and occupation a tract extending for ten miles on each side of the Minnesota between Lake Traverse and the Yellow Medicine River. Each of the thirty-five chiefs who signed received various gifts, but little of the actual money involved in the purchase ever reached their hands.

By noon the next day, tents had been struck and baggage packed, and the treaty makers had boarded a keelboat for the voyage downstream to a second treaty ground at Mendota. There, on August 5, meeting with the commissioners in the warehouse of the fur company, the Mdewakanton and Wahpekute bands sold their hereditary domain, which embraced much of the area bounded by the Mississippi below Fort Snelling on the east and the Minnesota and Blue Earth rivers on the west. Their reservation, twenty miles wide and some sixty miles long, extended on either side of the Minne-

BALLPLAYERS from Kaposia challenged the local Indians to a lacrosse game, and the resulting contest was one of the most spectacular events witnessed at the Traverse. Although they did not participate in the negotiations, these Mdewakanton Sioux and their chief, Little Crow, went to Traverse des Sioux with the treaty commissioners. The visiting lacrosse players, pictured at the right in the course of preparing for the game, painted their bodies and wore elaborate headdresses and highly ornamented breechcloths. *Water color by Mayer, 1898; courtesy Goucher College.*

81

sota between the mouths of the Yellow Medicine and Little Rock rivers. Each band was allowed ninety thousand dollars for its lands.

Almost a year was to pass before the Senate ratified the Minnesota treaties on June 23, 1852, and it became necessary to iron out many difficulties before payments to the Indians could be completed in October and November. This accomplished, the former western empire of the Sioux was at long last open for settlement. The Senate refused to ratify a third treaty negotiated in the autumn of 1851 by Governor Ramsey with the Chippewa at Pembina. Had it received official approval, this agreement would have made available to settlers some five million acres in the Red River Valley. It remained for a series of treaties signed between 1854 and 1866 to open the Chippewa lands of northern Minnesota, including the mining and lumbering areas of the east and the treeless agricultural paradise of the Red River country. These treaties, however, were more or less routine in character. The picturesque and dramatic events associated with the purchase of the Suland represent a unique chapter in Minnesota's history.

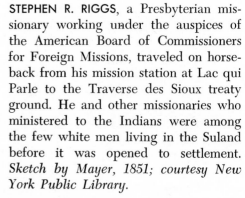

STEPHEN R. RIGGS, a Presbyterian missionary working under the auspices of the American Board of Commissioners for Foreign Missions, traveled on horseback from his mission station at Lac qui Parle to the Traverse des Sioux treaty ground. He and other missionaries who ministered to the Indians were among the few white men living in the Suland before it was opened to settlement. *Sketch by Mayer, 1851; courtesy New York Public Library.*

TRADERS and Indians alike enjoyed the leisurely, relaxed atmosphere of the camp at Traverse des Sioux while waiting for the tribesmen to arrive and the treaty negotiations to begin. *Sketch by Mayer, 1851; courtesy Newberry Library.*

THE SIGNING OF THE TREATY on July 23, 1851, brought to a dramatic climax the events of the previous weeks at Traverse des Sioux. The commissioners signed first, and then with great dignity thirty-five chiefs stepped forward, each in turn touching the pen with which Dr. Thomas Foster, the secretary, wrote the red leader's name. Many made short speeches, and as each signed, a presidential medal was placed around his neck and he was given blankets, tobacco, ammunition, trinkets, and other presents. To conclude the ceremony, the commissioner of Indian affairs made a valedictory speech. *Oil by Mayer, 1885.*

THE SKETCH at the right, on which Mayer based the oil reproduced above, was probably made by the artist during the treaty negotiations in 1851, while traders, commissioners, and Indians were assembled at Traverse des Sioux. *Courtesy New York Public Library.*

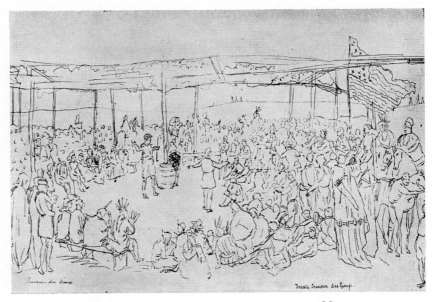

JAMES M. GOODHUE, editor of the *Minnesota Pioneer* published at St. Paul, went to Traverse des Sioux to report on the treaty negotiations for his newspaper. Although Mayer indicates that he pictured the journalist "as usual," his visit was fruitful, resulting in vivid descriptions of people and detailed day-by-day reports of events at the Traverse. *Sketch by Mayer, 1851; courtesy New York Public Library.*

A KEELBOAT carried some fifty people down the Minnesota from Traverse des Sioux to Fort Snelling near the second treaty ground of 1851 at Mendota. Among the passengers were the commissioners, traders, voyageurs, half-breeds, a few Indians, and other observers. "Four lusty voyageurs tugged at the oars"; another managed the stern oar; and Sibley served as captain. *Sketch by Mayer, 1851; courtesy New York Public Library.*

NIGHT ON THE KEELBOAT was enlivened by the voyageurs, who sang their traditional French airs and smoked to keep themselves awake for twenty-four hours before reaching Fort Snelling at noon on July 25. *Sketch by Mayer, 1851; courtesy New York Public Library.*

CHIEF LITTLE CROW of the Kaposia band, whose village was near the present site of South St. Paul, was the first Indian to sign the treaty of Mendota on August 5. He was splendidly dressed for the occasion and carried a peace pipe decorated with green duck feathers, porcupine quills, and human hair. Following him as signers were Chief Wabasha from a village near what is now Winona and various other headmen of the Lower Sioux. With the negotiation of the Mendota treaty, the sale of the Sioux empire to the white man was completed. *Portrait by Mayer, 1851; courtesy Newberry Library.*

10.

Homeseekers and Speculators

EAGER AND IMPATIENT LAND-SEEKERS crossed the Mississippi and occupied choice locations in the onetime empire of the Sioux even before the treaties of 1851 were ratified and proclaimed. Although thousands swarmed into the area before it was surveyed and the lands offered for sale in 1855, that year marked the beginning of the great rush into the trans-Mississippi country. Regardless of their destination, most of the settlers funneled through St. Paul. The season's first boat, the "War Eagle," which arrived on April 17, carried no fewer than 814 passengers. As the summer progressed, some days saw the arrival of as many as seven boats, each with its quota of land-hungry newcomers. The thousands who passed through the territorial capital taxed the resources of its hotels and boardinghouses and forced stage and boat owners to work their equipment to capacity. Population figures for the 1850s reflect a phenomenal growth. From a meager 4,535 in 1849, the territory's people increased to 40,000 in 1855, and then soared to 150,037 in 1857; and the census of 1860 credited Minnesota with 172,023 inhabitants.

The westward rush into the new territory was not entirely spontaneous. Apparently aware of the value of advertising, the Minnesota legislators of 1853 appropriated three hundred dollars for a Minnesota display at the Crystal Palace Exhibition in New York City. To install the exhibit, William G. Le Duc went east, taking with him such characteristic items as a birch-bark canoe, a Red River cart, and a live buffalo bull, in addition to products typical of Minnesota and pictures of the area. Although the fair management refused permission to display the buffalo, visitors to the exhibition doubtless learned something about the new territory.

In 1855 the legislature took more direct steps to attract settlers. It provided for an emigration commissioner who would live in New York, meet incoming ships, and tell newly arrived immigrants about the glories of the Minnesota country. Eugene Burnand, who was named to the position, operated chiefly among incoming Germans and

Belgians. How much credit he should receive for the increase in the number of Minnesota's Germans from 147 in 1850 to 18,400 in 1860 would be difficult to determine. Without Burnand's encouragement the new state's Scandinavian population showed an astounding growth, multiplying from 12 to nearly 12,000 in the same decade.

Yankee migration, too, was gaining rapidly in momentum, stimulated no doubt by newspaper editors both in Minnesota and in the East who filled column after column with enthusiastic reports of the beauty, the productivity, and the healthfulness of the new region. One editor, in fact, predicted that Minnesota was destined to "become the New England of the West." Organized colonies, composed of individuals bound for a single locality, attracted other groups to the territory. Rolling Stone, planned by a New York association in 1852, centered about Minnesota City near Winona; the substantial German community of New Ulm grew out of the colonizing activities of Germans in Chicago and Cincinnati; groups of New England families established communities at Zumbrota and Excelsior; and English colonists transplanted the customs of their homeland to Fairmont.

Many of the newcomers who acquired farms or town lots in Minnesota in the 1850s were homeseekers, interested in settling permanently in the new territory. Under the pre-emption laws, they could buy surveyed public lands for $1.25 per acre at United States land offices located at Stillwater, Minneapolis, Winona, Red Wing, Chatfield, Sauk Rapids, and other scattered points. In addition to actual settlers, hordes of speculators patronized these western land offices, pre-empting tracts on which to establish townsites. After preparing appropriate town plats, these frontier real-estate operators proceeded to sell lots at inflated figures, often reaping enormous profits on minute investments. Some of the boom towns thus founded developed into substantial communities, but many of them existed only on paper. It has been estimated that between 1854 and 1857 some seven hundred towns were platted in Minnesota with lots enough to accommodate a million and a half people.

Typical Minnesota townsite speculators of the 1850s were John H. Stevens, who in 1849 built the first house in the area where five years later he platted Minneapolis, and an associate named Edwin Whitefield. They organized the Kandiyohi Town Site Company in October, 1856, and Whitefield employed his considerable talents both as an artist and an author to advertise the project. By contributing articles to such widely read publications as the *New York Tribune* and *Harper's* and *Leslie's* magazines, and giving illustrated lectures before audiences in various eastern population centers, Whitefield attracted the attention of both settlers and investors. He also displayed collections of his pictures at the Minnesota territorial fair of 1856 and in cities of the East. Hundreds of Whitefield's striking water colors of Minnesota scenes and a number of lithographs, all based on sketches made in the field between 1856 and 1859, have survived, providing a fresh and authentic visual record of the frontier he was striving to exploit while pioneering as an advertising artist.

Some of Whitefield's townsite projects, like Glencoe, prospered and persisted; others,

TOWNSITE PROMOTERS often lived in the field for weeks on end, surveying lands and selecting locations for new communities. These explorers for the Kandiyohi Town Site Company were encamped on Lake Lillian, which was named for Mrs. Whitefield, wife of the artist who painted this water color in 1856.

like Karns City and Kandota, failed to develop. With hundreds of additional boom towns—among them Nininger near Hastings—they fell victim to the panic of 1857, which was marked in Minnesota by a sharp drop in land values. The latter townsite, planned by Governor Ramsey's speculating brother-in-law, John Nininger, has special interest because it attracted to Minnesota a young lawyer named Ignatius Donnelly. Nininger failed to match the dreams of its founders, but Donnelly remained to become one of the state's most renowned citizens.

The financial panic notwithstanding, by the end of 1857 Minnesota was dotted with well-established communities and farms and was occupied by a population sufficient for statehood. Many of the towns hugged the banks of the Mississippi opposite the Wisconsin shore—Homer, Winona, Wabasha, Read's Landing, Frontenac, Red Wing, Hastings. St. Paul was firmly established at the head of navigation, and the twin towns of St. Anthony and Minneapolis were growing rapidly at the falls. Upstream, near Sauk Rapids, St. Cloud had a foothold, and along the course of the Minnesota River such towns as Shakopee, St. Peter, and New Ulm were beginning to develop. There were signs of permanent settlement, too, far to the north on the future sites of Duluth and Beaver Bay along Lake Superior's shore. Peopled largely by homeseekers of the 1850s, these scattered Minnesota settlements looked forward to statehood with confident expectations.

88

A SHARE OF STOCK in Karns City was valued at $200, according to this certificate made out to Stevens and signed by S. D. Karns. *From the John H. Stevens Papers.*

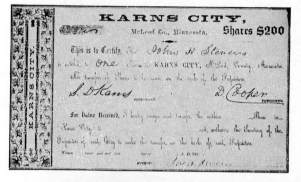

THE KANDIYOHI TOWN SITE COMPANY was typical of hundreds of groups operating in Minnesota in the mid-1850s. Among its members pictured above at work in the field were Stevens and Karns. *Water color by Whitefield, 1856.*

KARNS CITY, on Lake Marion, one of a chain of waters in western McLeod County, was among the townsites founded by the Kandiyohi group. It was laid out in September, 1856, and was named for Karns, one of twenty-two members who signed the constitution of the company. *Water color by Whitefield, 1856; courtesy Chicago Historical Society.*

KANDOTA in Todd County near Sauk Centre, pictured above, was one of Whitefield's favorite townsites. He was partial to the Sauk River Valley, declaring in 1858 that it "has been very correctly termed 'The Farmer's Paradise.'" *Water color by Whitefield, 1857.*

NININGER, a widely advertised townsite laid out in the summer of 1856, attracted from five hundred to a thousand settlers before the inflationary bubble burst during the panic of 1857. At the peak of its boom, lots in this town sold for from $200 to $250 each. *From a scrapbook kept by Ignatius Donnelly.*

EMIGRATION

UP THE MISSISSIPPI RIVER.

The attention of Emigrants and the Public generally, is called to the now rapidly improving

TERRITORY OF MINNESOTA,

Containing a population of 150,000, and goes into the Union as a State during the present year. According to an act of Congress passed last February, the State is munificently endowed with Lands for Public Schools and State Universities, also granting five per cent. on all sales of U. S. Lands for Internal Improvements. On the 3d March, 1857, grants of Land from Congress was made to the leading Trunk Railroads in Minnesota, so that in a short time the trip from New Orleans to any part of the State will be made in from two and a half to three days. The

CITY OF NININGER,

Situated on the Mississippi River, 35 miles below St. Paul, is now a prominent point for a large Commercial Town, being backed by an extensive Agricultural, Grazing and Farming Country; has fine streams in the interior, well adapted for Milling in all its branches; and Manufacturing WATER POWER to any extent.

Mr. JOHN NININGER, (a Gentleman of large means, ideas and liberality, speaking the various languages,) is the principal Proprietor of Nininger. He laid it out on such principles as to encourage all MECHANICS, Merchants, or Professions of all kinds, on the same equality and footing: the consequence is, the place has gone ahead with such rapidity that it is now an established City, and will annually double in population for years to come.

Persons arriving by Ship or otherwise, can be transferred without expense to Steamers going to Saint Louis; or stop at Cairo, and take Railroad to Dunleith (on the Mississippi). Steamboats leave Saint Louis and Dunleith daily for NININGER, and make the trip from Dunleith in 36 to 48 hours.

NOTICES.

1. All Railroads and Steamboats giving this card a conspicuous place, or *gratuitous insertion* in their cards, AIDS THE EMIGRANT and forwards their own interest.

2. For authentic documents, reliable information, and all particulars in regard to Occupations, Wages, Preëmpting Lands (in neighborhood), Lumber, Price of Lots, Expenses, &c., apply to

THOMAS B. WINSTON, 27 Camp street, New Orleans.
ROBERT CAMPBELL, St. Louis.
JOSEPH B. FORBES, Dunleith.

HOMER (left), on the Mississippi below Winona, was platted in 1855 by Willard B. Bunnell. His house is now owned by the Winona County Historical Society. *Water color by John L. Sperry, 1869; courtesy New York State Historical Association, Cooperstown.*

90

WINONA was platted in June, 1852, on a tract long known as Wabasha Prairie for the Sioux chief who lived there earlier. Because it was subject to flooding, promoters avoided the location until Captain Orrin Smith of the steamboat "Nominee" hired Erwin F. Johnson to occupy it, landing him there with two woodcutters on the night of October 15, 1851. They built the first claim shanty in what became Winona, which developed into the most substantial river town in Minnesota below St. Paul. *Photograph taken in 1861.*

RED WING bears the name of the Sioux chief whose village was located at the foot of the spectacular Barn Bluff. An Indian mission and a trading post existed there before the first homeseeker, John Day, staked a claim in the vicinity in 1852. *Water color by Whitefield, about 1857.*

91

SHAKOPEE on the Minnesota River was platted in 1854 on the site of a Sioux village and Indian trading post. It was named for the chief whose band lived there before the treaties of 1851. *Water color by Whitefield, 1858.*

NEW ULM was founded in 1856 by German immigrants from Chicago and Cincinnati who organized a colony for the purpose of settling on the Minnesota River. These people were seeking a spot where they could practice liberalism in religion and politics. The social life of the new community was centered in its Turnverein. *Lithograph, 1860.*

BEAVER BAY on Lake Superior was platted in 1856 near the mouth of the Beaver River on land opened to settlement by a treaty with the Chippewa signed two years earlier at La Pointe. *Oil by a Mrs. Lowry, a north shore pioneer, about 1870; courtesy St. Louis County Historical Society, Duluth.*

ST. PAUL, on the east side of the Mississippi at the head of navigation, had developed into a thriving community before the west bank of the river was opened to settlement. By 1850 it had a population of 1,294 living in 384 dwellings, and seven years later some 10,000 people resided in the growing territorial capital. *Water color by Jean Baptist Wengler, 1851; courtesy Landesmuseum, Linz, Austria.*

ST. ANTHONY AND MINNEAPOLIS bordered both banks of the Mississippi in the vicinity of the falls by the close of the territorial era. The older and larger St. Anthony had 4,689 people, while its neighbor to the west had a population of only 3,391 in 1857. In the same year the towns were connected by two bridges, but that in the left background collapsed when spring floods piled logs against it in 1859. *Photograph by Upton, 1857.*

93

11.

Frontier Economy

ALTHOUGH THE DECADE of the 1850s was strongly characterized by land specu-
lation, it also was an era of economic progress during which the foundations for future prosperity were laid. As the trader's frontier was replaced by that of the settler,
the latter's needs gave rise to a new economy involving manufactured goods, merchan-
dising, financing, and professional services. Logging and lumber processing increased
in response to the newcomers' demands for building materials; more and more merchants arrived by steamboat with stocks of goods ranging from clothing to coffee and
from books to jewelry, which they offered for sale in shops and wholesale establishments; hotels were built to accommodate ever-increasing numbers of transients; professional people, including lawyers, civil engineers, journalists, physicians, and dentists
responded to the demands for their services by settling in the area's expanding centers
of population; banks were established; and real-estate dealers by the score opened offices to conduct land sales and exchanges.

Topping the list of products manufactured in Minnesota in the 1850s was lumber,
with 185 sawmills in operation by June of 1860. Some of it was converted at factories
into such needed articles as doors, sashes, shingles, furniture, barrels, pails, and matches.
Flour mills, breweries, tanneries, and foundries also were operating in appreciable
numbers. Among locally manufactured items much in demand for frontier consump-
tion were agricultural implements, wagons, shoes, saddles, tin, sheet iron, bricks, brooms,
pottery, and cigars. Although many manufacturing plants were concentrated in St.
Paul, St. Anthony, and Minneapolis, they were to be found also at such places as Anoka,
Chatfield, New Ulm, Winona, Faribault, Carver, and Preston.

That many of those who purchased land in the 1850s remained to live and work
on it is evidenced by the growing number of Minnesota farms. From a meager 157
at the beginning of the decade, the figure rose to 18,081 in 1860. Settlers began to heed
the advice of boosters who predicted that an ample "market for all that can be raised

94

THE SAWMILL built at Marine Mills on the St. Croix in 1839 had developed into a substantial plant by the 1850s. Minnesota lumbermen not only had easy access to a plentiful supply of timber, but they enjoyed the advantages of good water power for turning logs into lumber and convenient streams on which to float rafts southward to expanding markets. *Stereograph by J. P. Doremus; courtesy James Taylor Dunn, St. Paul.*

in Minnesota" would exist for years to come and that produce would command high prices. By the end of the decade, locally grown food was to some extent replacing that brought in by boat, and the winter shortages that accompanied the freezing of the Mississippi were becoming less acute. Crops like potatoes, corn, and oats attained importance in the 1850s; dairy products soared in value from eleven hundred dollars in 1850 to more than three million in 1860; livestock raising became significant, and the meat-packing industry gained a foothold with twenty-two plants in operation by the end of the decade. To supplement their incomes, farmers exploited native products like maple sugar, cranberries, and ginseng.

Most important of all for Minnesota's future prosperity was the increase in wheat raising, which was stimulated by the need for flour. When the Island Mills opened at the Falls of St. Anthony in 1854, the supply of local wheat was insufficient to keep the plant running, and it had to buy some of its grain down river and ship it in by steamboat. As Minnesota farmers responded to the demand for wheat, however, more and more flour mills were built, and by the end of the decade eighty-five were to be found in such scattered localities as Marine, Northfield, Dundas, Hastings, and Winona, in addition to St. Anthony, Minneapolis, and St. Paul. Some of these early mills produced a surplus for shipment to eastern markets.

Minnesota's growing population demanded more than food. In 1860 clothing could

95

A FLOUR MILL, built about 1853 at the falls of the Vermillion River near Hastings and acquired in 1856 by William G. Le Duc, is pictured in this photograph taken in 1859. At the lower falls of the same stream, Governor Ramsey and Dr. Thomas Foster erected a mill in 1857.

FARMS like this one in Wabasha County produced the wheat ground in the small flour and grist mills built at water-power sites throughout southern Minnesota in the 1850s. *Photograph taken about 1875; courtesy Mrs. F. W. Gerber, Plainview.*

96

ARD GODFREY is typical of the Yankees who migrated to Minnesota from Maine. He built the first log dam at the Falls of St. Anthony in 1847, and two years later he helped erect the first commercial sawmill there.

ST. ANTHONY in 1857 had this large sawmill and the small gristmill at the extreme left. Power for both was provided by the St. Anthony Falls Water Power Company, organized in 1856 by Steele and others. *Photograph by Upton, 1857.*

be purchased in twenty St. Paul and six Minneapolis shops, and the Minnesota capital boasted eleven jewelers and five booksellers. The number of newspapers increased rapidly after James M. Goodhue established the territory's first paper, the *Minnesota Pioneer*, at St. Paul in 1849. By 1859 six papers were being published in the capital city—four in English, one in German, and another in Norwegian; in the same year, St. Anthony had three papers and Minneapolis, four. Encouraged by the pioneers' desire to send likenesses to far-off friends and relatives, five daguerreotypists opened studios in St. Paul in the 1850s, and two each established themselves in St. Anthony and Minneapolis. The need for capital and the resulting high interest rates attracted bankers, whose financial operations frequently included dealings in real estate. Although only three St. Paul banks survived the panic of 1857, a year later the number had grown to fourteen. Among professional men, attorneys were the most numerous. In 1859, fifty-two were living in St. Paul, twenty-four in Minneapolis, and fourteen in St. Anthony. Physicians came next, with twenty practicing in St. Paul, eleven in Minneapolis, and ten in St. Anthony.

The need for temporary accommodations by settlers who could afford to pay for lodging while waiting for more permanent living quarters, as well as by visitors, investors, and other transients, stimulated the building of hotels. During a single week in the autumn of 1856, no fewer than a thousand guests were crowded into St. Paul hostelries. Most of them were extremely simple and often downright uncomfortable. A pioneer St. Paul housewife who was obliged to live at the American House during her first months of residence in the frontier town complained that the quarters were cramped and the food monotonous, consisting largely of bacon, potatoes, and tea. The St. Paul city directory of 1858 listed twenty-five hotels, some of which offered greatly improved accommodations. Perhaps the best-equipped and most elaborate of the new establishments was the Fuller House built at Seventh and Jackson streets in 1856 by Alpheus G. Fuller. It included parlors, a reception room, a washroom, and a "magnificent saloon," and its guests enjoyed such conveniences as steam heat and "home-manufactured gas." The Winslow House, erected in St. Anthony in 1857, catered to Southerners who traveled up the Mississippi in search of cool northern summers. It boasted the "most capacious and beautiful" ballroom west of Chicago, and its dining room was said to seat five hundred people. The Nicollet House, opened in the spring of 1858 in Minneapolis, was that city's most elaborate hostelry.

Of prime importance in the economy of the frontier was transportation. The majority of the settlers who reached Minnesota in the 1850s, as well as most of the supplies they needed, came by steamboat. In the first year of the decade, only five boats were engaged in the upper Mississippi trade and 104 arrivals were recorded at St. Paul, the head of navigation. Later the St. Paul levee became the destination of most of the steamboats that pushed northward on the Father of Waters. By 1858, the number of boats had increased to 62, and the arrivals at St. Paul reached a total of 1,090. In an

THE ISLAND MILLS, erected at the Falls of St. Anthony in 1854 at a cost of $16,000, were equipped with three pairs of millstones. This daguerreotype of the interior, taken about 1858, shows millers Francis and J. P. Hill at work.

PRODUCTION of pails and tubs began at the Falls of St. Anthony in the 1850s. This factory also was equipped for "planing, matching, and splitting" lumber. *Photograph taken about 1860.*

ST. ANTHONY'S SKY LINE was dominated by its largest hotel, the Winslow House, in the mid-1850s. It loomed above the falls, the mills, and the wooden bridge which connected the town with Nicollet Island. *Oil by Ferdinand Pritchardt, 1856.*

average season, the river was open for navigation 222 days between early April and late November.

Steamboat traffic was important also in other parts of Minnesota. Before landing at St. Paul, boats from below often ascended the St. Croix as far as Stillwater. Although the Falls of St. Anthony constituted a barrier beyond which boats from Galena and St. Louis could not pass, it marked a starting point for other smaller craft, like the "Governor Ramsey," which pushed as far north as Sauk Rapids and Little Falls. On the Minnesota River, steamboating was stimulated first by the building of Fort Ridgely and the establishment of the Sioux agencies in 1853, and later by the settlement of the area. Many of the boats engaged in that trade also plied the Mississippi. Among them was the "West Newton," which carried troops and supplies to Fort Ridgely in April, 1853. Pork, flour, and gold for Indian payments were included in its cargo. From a meager beginning in 1851, when three boats from the Minnesota River landed at St. Paul, traffic on that stream increased rapidly in volume until 394 landings were recorded in 1858 and 413 in 1862.

Steamboat transportation developed last on the Red River, where Anson Northup launched the first vessel in 1859, giving it his own name. J. C. Burbank and Company of St. Paul soon purchased the boat, renaming it the "Pioneer," and in 1861 the same firm put the "International" into operation on the stream that flows northward across the boundary to Canada.

To make connections with its river transports, the Burbank firm established a stage line between St. Cloud and Breckenridge. The combined boat and stage traffic soon began to replace the picturesque Red River cart trade, which by 1858 had reached impressive proportions. From a modest beginning in 1844, when six carts traversed the rough trails between the Red River Settlements and St. Paul, the traffic grew until the caravan of 1858 consisted of some six hundred carts. In a single year, their mixed-blood drivers transported to St. Paul from the area between Pembina and Fort Garry furs valued at $182,491. The Red River traders spent in the Minnesota capital much of the money obtained for the pelts they sold, loading their carts with groceries, tobacco, dry goods, clothing, and other articles before returning to their northern homes. As a result of this trade, St. Paul developed into an important wholesale fur market; five fur dealers had establishments there by 1859.

The Red River trails over which the crude wooden carts of the traders passed each summer may be considered Minnesota's earliest roads. As stagecoaches began to carry mail and passengers, however, the need for roads that could be used in all seasons became evident. Hundreds were laid out and surveyed during the 1850s, and with federal and territorial aid a network was developed in southern Minnesota. Stage lines

A CLOTHING STORE was opened at Third and Cedar streets in St. Paul by Charles D. Elfelt, a pioneer of 1849. Joel E. Whitney, who doubtless took this picture about 1855, operated the Sky Light Daguerrean Gallery above the store. Christ Church and the dome of the Ramsey County Courthouse can be seen in the background.

BOOK, drug, and clothing stores, and a lawyer's office were housed in Spooner's Building on Main Street in St. Anthony. Entertainments were staged upstairs in Cataract Hall. *Daguerreotype by A. W. Monell, about 1855.*

connected such points as Stillwater, St. Anthony, and St. Paul with towns to the south, west, and north—among them communities as far away as Monticello and Crow Wing. Stagecoaches met boats as they docked at the St. Paul levee to convey passengers to local hotels and neighboring towns. Ferries, chartered and established to carry vehicles and pedestrians across streams, were in time replaced by bridges. The earliest to span the Mississippi was the picturesque Suspension Bridge completed in 1855 between Nicollet Island and Minneapolis at a cost of fifty thousand dollars. A crude bridge between the island and St. Anthony made possible the entire crossing from St. Anthony to Minneapolis. At St. Paul, a bridge connecting the foot of Wabasha Street and the west side of the Mississippi was completed in 1859.

Before the decade of the 1850s came to a close, Minnesotans were looking forward to rail transportation. They had their earliest tastes of its advantages in 1854 and 1858, when roads were completed to Rock Island and La Crosse on the Mississippi. Jubilant railroad builders celebrated these events by arranging elaborate river excursions between their road's western terminal and the head of navigation in Minnesota. A premature attempt to build railways within Minnesota ended disastrously. More than twenty roads were chartered by the territorial legislature, which on the eve of statehood authorized several to issue bonds backed by state credit to the extent of five million dollars. The railroads went bankrupt, however, partly as a result of the panic of 1857. Minnesotans were obliged to wait until 1862 for their first railroad, and it was not until 1867 that they could enjoy the economic advantages of a direct rail connection with Chicago and the eastern seaboard.

A PRIVATE BANK operated by Truman M. Smith was located on the ground floor of the Fuller House, a St. Paul hotel. The panic of 1857 forced Smith to suspend payment in October, and thereafter he devoted his energies to real estate. *Wood engraving, about 1856.*

BANKERS at St. Anthony included O. Curtis, who advertised in the *Minnesota Republican* of July 30, 1857, that he loaned and invested money, bought and sold real estate and land warrants, and handled business for nonresidents.

101

JAMES M. GOODHUE, who arrived in St. Paul on April 18, 1849, issued the first Minnesota newspaper ten days later. Before his death in August, 1852, he became a force in territorial politics and gained a reputation as an enthusiastic booster for his adopted community.

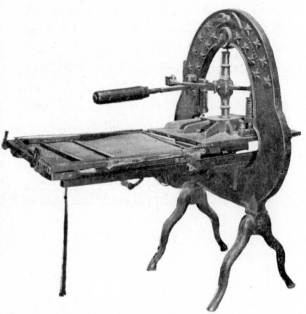

THIS WASHINGTON HAND PRESS, in the museum of the Minnesota Historical Society, is similar to that used by Goodhue in printing the early issues of the *Pioneer*.

THE PUBLICATION OFFICE of the *Pioneer* was located at Third and Jackson streets from 1854 to 1859. In 1855 the paper joined forces with the *Minnesota Democrat*, founded in 1850. The name was changed to the *St. Paul Pioneer* in 1862, and the paper still exists as the *St. Paul Pioneer Press*. *Photograph taken about 1856.*

DR. THOMAS R. POTTS, a pioneer physician, settled in St. Paul in 1849. He was the first president of the Minnesota State Medical Society, which was organized by eleven physicians in July, 1853, and was later city physician and health officer of St. Paul. *Daguerreotype taken about 1850.*

BRADLEY B. MEEKER, frontier jurist, was appointed to the supreme court of Minnesota Territory in 1849. He presided over the first term of court on the west bank of the Mississippi at the Falls of St. Anthony in August, 1849. *Photograph by Mathew Brady, about 1860; courtesy National Archives.*

RICHARD CHUTE, who with his wife settled in Minneapolis in 1854, played a major role in developing the water power of the Falls of St. Anthony. *Photograph probably taken in the 1850s.*

JOHN W. NORTH, a lawyer who settled at St. Anthony in 1849, helped to organize the Republican party in Minnesota and, in 1856, founded the city of Northfield. *Daguerreotype taken in 1856.*

GALENA, ILLINOIS, was the starting point for steamboat trips to the upper Mississippi until 1854, when a railroad was completed to Rock Island. The "Nominee," here shown at the Galena levee, was among the boats that carried thousands of settlers to Minnesota. *Daguerreotype taken in 1852, probably by Alexander Hesler; courtesy Chicago Historical Society.*

THE ST. PAUL LEVEE is pictured above in 1858, the peak year for the upper Mississippi trade. The season opened on March 25 with the landing of the "Grey Eagle," the first boat at the left in this group. The length of the St. Paul shipping season was controlled by the thawing and freezing of Lake Pepin.

THE "ANSON NORTHUP," the first steamboat on the Red River, was designed with an extremely shallow draft for navigation of that winding stream. *From Samuel H. Scudder,* The Winnipeg Country *(Boston, 1886).*

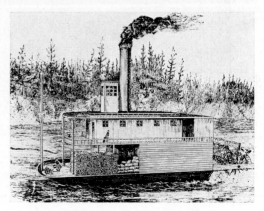

104

THE RED RIVER CART train pictured at left was arriving in St. Paul with a cargo of furs, after a journey of about five hundred miles from Pembina or Fort Garry. Thirty to forty days were needed for such trips over rough trails via Fort Abercrombie and St. Cloud or Otter Tail Lake and Crow Wing. *Photograph by Whitney, 1850s.*

THE TRAIN of Red River carts pictured at the right was ready for the return journey to the north country. Arriving in St. Paul in July, 1859, it carried pelts valued at $150,000. Most numerous among the furs transported were buffalo robes and muskrat, beaver, and raccoon skins. Much of this cargo eventually reached New York City and London.

THE STAGECOACHES and other vehicles shown in the photograph at the left were lined up in front of the American House, St. Paul, in 1856. They probably belonged to a near-by livery which ran stages to St. Anthony twice a day and to Fort Ripley once a week. By 1858 a St. Paul firm was running daily stages to seven towns; among them were Anoka, St. Cloud, and Little Falls.

A SUSPENSION BRIDGE, which was the first span across the Mississippi anywhere along its course, replaced the ferry between Minneapolis and Nicollet Island in 1855. Tolls amounting to twenty-five cents for a horse and buggy and five cents for each passenger brought in an average of fifty dollars a day the first year and seventy-five the second. According to contemporary reports, the structure cost $36,000. *Daguerreotype taken in the 1850s.*

FERRIES were usually established wherever early roads crossed major streams. Scores were chartered by the territorial legislature, and the holder of a charter at a busy crossing often accumulated substantial profits in fees. This ferry, across the St. Croix at Marine, was used until 1954. *Photograph by John W. G. Dunn, 1917.*

106

12.

Social and
Cultural Frontiers

AS THE SUPPLY of economic goods increased and transportation became less difficult, life in Minnesota lost some of its simple frontier flavor. Social and cultural conditions, too, improved in the 1850s, taking on the characteristics of the areas from which
the pioneer settlers came. Home life was quick to reflect the expanding economy of the
new territory on the upper Mississippi. The firstcomers used materials at hand, building houses and barns of logs in the wooded areas of southeastern Minnesota. As late as
1851, log cabins still were in evidence in the St. Paul business district. Frame and brick
buildings gradually replaced these structures as the products of local sawmills and
brickyards became more generally available. When the treeless regions of western Minnesota were occupied, ingenious settlers used the prairie sod as building material, and
sod houses and barns became a common feature of frontier life. Stone, too, gained in
popularity, and many an early St. Paul structure utilized limestone from local quarries.

By 1860 certain home conveniences were available in Minnesota, particularly in St.
Paul, the business metropolis and cultural center of the new commonwealth. The house
built in that year by Horace Thompson was fully equipped with gas and water, and was
centrally heated from a basement furnace. In the 1850s, however, such innovations
were the exception rather than the rule. Tallow dips and candles furnished light for
most frontier families; even kerosene lamps did not come into use until 1859, and then
they were usually sold by druggists. Water was obtained chiefly from springs or wells,
and in 1856 a "wheelbarrow man" was selling this necessary article to St. Paul residents.
Open fireplaces and wood stoves usually were used both for heating and cooking, though
some of the more pretentious homes had decorative "mantles of marbleized iron" or
marble chimney pieces. Wood for fuel was cheap and plentiful, and after the St. Paul
Gas Company began to operate its plant in 1857, it sold coke for twenty-five cents a
bushel. In the same year, the city was completely piped for gas, and street lamps were
installed in the business section.

Many a frontier housewife brought treasured furnishings and table appointments to Minnesota from the East or from Europe, but as the decade of the 1850s advanced, household articles became available in local shops. St. Paul pioneers had access to a furniture store as early as 1853, and by 1858 the number had increased to five. Residents of St. Anthony and Minneapolis could buy from two furniture dealers in each city by 1859, not to mention a cabinetmaker who doubled as undertaker for the latter community. In selecting furniture, "comfort was the first consideration" of the pioneer homemaker; "sofas and chairs were chosen with that in view," according to Governor Ramsey's daughter, who vividly recalled the Minnesota home of her childhood. She remembered that "A few pictures hung high on the walls," and that the "ornaments all collected on the étagère or whatnot were really negligible in the general effect." And yet, she recalled, the "whole atmosphere of the rooms was one of cozy, homelike cheer." Just such an atmosphere is reflected in the few known pictures of Minnesota interiors of the 1850s.

A rapidly increasing number of grocers, bakers, and butchers catered to pioneers in the larger settlements. One St. Paul mother of 1855 found food supplies inadequate until she discovered that she could purchase such items as butter, cheese, milk, and vegetables at a public market. It was established in 1853 for the benefit of farmers who had surplus produce to sell. The territorial capital, however, did not lack food stores. It had ten grocers in 1853, and by 1858 the community's housewives could stock their larders with purchases from forty-four grocery stores, eight bakeries, nineteen butcher shops, and five confectionery stores. Food preservation by refrigeration was not unknown. In 1851 St. Paul had an icehouse large enough to store nine hundred tons of ice cut during the winter months.

Although the average pioneer family lived on a diet consisting mainly of potatoes, pork, and corn bread, occasionally varied by fish, venison, and other game, elaborate banquets marked special occasions. Luxuries in great array seem to have found their

THE LOG HOUSE era overlapped that of the hoop skirt in Minnesota, as illustrated by this picture of Robert Orrock and members of his family posing beside their Sherburne County cabin in 1857. *Photograph by Upton.*

THIS SOD HOUSE near Madison in Lac qui Parle County was typical of those built by settlers in western Minnesota. *Photograph taken about 1875; courtesy Lac qui Parle County Historical Society, Madison.*

SUBSTANTIAL MANSIONS, like this residence built of local limestone at Hastings in the late 1850s by William Gates Le Duc, were beginning to appear in Minnesota communities by the close of the decade. The Victorian Gothic house was acquired in 1931 by Mr. Carroll B. Simmons, who assured its permanent preservation by presenting it to the Minnesota Historical Society in 1958. *Photograph by Robert C. Wheeler, 1958.*

FURNISHINGS selected for comfort and convenience rather than beauty characterized the St. Paul home of the Reverend E. D. Neill and his family in the 1850s. The corner whatnot loaded with ornaments was typical of the period, and the books reflect the cultural interests of these pioneers. *Stereograph taken about 1858; courtesy Misses Furness.*

FURNITURE manufactured in the East and the South was shipped upstream by steamboat and unloaded at the St. Paul levee for transfer to stores in the Minnesota capital and neighboring communities. Also available in frontier furniture marts were chairs, sofas, tables, bedroom suites, and many other items produced locally by pioneer cabinetmakers. *Photograph by W. H. Illingworth, about 1865.*

THREE FRONTIER HOMEMAKERS of the 1850s are pictured above. At the left is Amelia Ullmann of St. Paul, who in 1857 sat for this portrait by Thomas C. Healy of Chicago. In the center is a daguerreotype of Ann Loomis North, who was the proud owner of one of the earliest pianos in St. Anthony. Anna Jenks Ramsey posed for the photograph at the right, probably in the 1850s. A woman of great charm and tact, she presided at social functions as the governor's lady, entertaining residents of and visitors to the frontier capital.

way to holiday dinner tables. A hundred people who attended a Christmas fair in St. Paul in December, 1851, sat down to a supper of oyster and lobster soup, turkeys, chickens, frosted hams, buffalo tongues, ice cream, and "piquants." Turkeys, shipped by sleigh from Iowa and Illinois, sold that winter for $1.50 and $2.00 each. For a festival held at the Fuller House in St. Paul on December 22, 1856, to mark the anniversary of the landing of the Pilgrims, the menu included mock turtle soup, several kinds of fish, chicken, turkey, tongue, veal, pork, lamb, venison, twenty different kinds of pastries, nuts, raisins, fruit, and ice cream.

Local products like buffalo tongues, which were considered a great delicacy, venison, and cranberries frequently appeared on pioneer dinner tables. When Mrs. Ramsey entertained, she often served smoked buffalo tongue along with more conventional fare like chicken and lobster salads, scalloped oysters, and beaten biscuits. On some occasions the governor's lady was called upon to entertain distinguished visitors on extremely short notice. Then her neighbors came to her assistance, each baking or cooking her own specialty for the reception. Although Anna Ramsey was only twenty-two years old when she arrived in Minnesota with her husband, she soon gained a reputation as a frontier hostess of great charm and poise.

Social activities of the 1850s did not always center in hotels and homes. Among

110

other quarters soon available for parties and various types of entertainment was the popular Mazourka Hall above the Elfelt brothers' St. Paul dry goods store. Classic paintings "representing the Nine Muses" adorned the walls, forming a background for lectures, concerts, and dramatic entertainments. Parties were held there every Thursday evening in the winter of 1850–51. Residents of St. Anthony flocked to Cataract Hall in December, 1855, for a series of cotillion parties. It was first used in June, 1854, for a showing of Prentiss' "Panorama of the Crystal Palace of New York." When these gathering places proved too cramped, entertainers sometimes performed in the House chamber of the Minnesota Capitol, and occasionally a church made its auditorium available for a lecture.

Houses of worship multiplied rapidly in the 1850s, and many denominations were represented. At least fifteen congregations were holding services in St. Paul in 1859; in the same year, Minneapolis had eight and St. Anthony seven churches. Most numerous were Episcopal, Presbyterian, Methodist, Baptist, Congregational, and Catholic congregations. Lutheran churches were established as early as 1854 in such centers of Scandinavian settlement as the Chisago Lake area and Vasa. Represented also were the Quakers, who assembled for regular meetings in Minneapolis in the mid-1850s; the Jews, who held their first services in St. Paul in 1856 and organized a congregation in the following year; and the Universalists in St. Anthony. Separate German and Norwegian Methodist congregations were active in the capital city, which also had German Lutheran and Catholic churches.

TWO PIONEER ST. PAUL CHURCHES, the First Presbyterian (left) at Third and St. Peter streets, and Christ Episcopal (right) on Cedar Street, were organized by Neill and James Lloyd Breck in 1849 and 1850 respectively. *Water colors by Wengler, 1851, in the Landesmuseum, Linz.*

111

THE FIRST CATHEDRAL OF ST. PAUL, erected on St. Peter Street in 1852 under Bishop Cretin's direction, replaced Father Galtier's log chapel. The first floor was used as a school and the second as a church. *Courtesy St. Paul Seminary.*

THE RIGHT REVEREND JOSEPH CRETIN arrived in St. Paul to serve as its first Catholic bishop in 1851. *Ambrotype taken in the 1850s; courtesy St. Paul Seminary.*

In a town "that boasts of half a dozen steepled churches," complained Goodhue referring to St. Paul in the *Pioneer* of March 27, 1851, "there is not a building . . . fit to be called a District school house. The only building known as such is hardly fit for a horse stable." Although the city's public schools were organized in 1849, it was not until eight years later that the first schoolhouse was erected under the auspices of the local board of education. By 1859 the city had three public schools, each with separate boys' and girls' grammar departments, as well as primary and intermediate sections. Under a legislative act of 1856, St. Paul became the first school district in the territory. The Reverend Edward D. Neill, a pioneer Presbyterian minister, was named secretary of the board of education and superintendent of schools. One of his contributions was a design for a seal. St. Anthony had three district schools by 1860, and Minneapolis could boast of its large Central Union School.

NEILL based his design for the seal of the St. Paul board of education on this photograph of himself and his son Samuel, which was taken about 1856.

Private and church schools were established in various localities throughout the territorial era. One of the earliest was opened in 1847 in a "mud-walled log hovel" once used as a blacksmith shop in St. Paul. Its founder, Harriet Bishop, later established a "Female Seminary" in a brick building erected for the purpose after the city's first district school opened. Another school for girls, founded by the Reverend J. G. Riheldaffer in 1858, attracted pupils from many Minnesota communities and from such far-off states as New York and Louisiana. The Baldwin School opened in 1853 with an initial enrollment of twenty-eight boys and forty-three girls. Neill was president of this institution, which eventually was reorganized as Macalester College.

Under a charter from the territorial legislature, Hamline University opened a preparatory department at Red Wing in 1854. This Methodist school, which later moved to St. Paul, was only one of a number established in frontier Minnesota by religious denominations. The Catholics opened parochial schools in connection with the Cathedral and with Assumption Church in St. Paul, as well as through the Benedictines, who established schools in St. Cloud which in the course of a century have developed as St. John's University at Collegeville and the College of St. Benedict at St. Joseph. Under Episcopal auspices, Shattuck School for boys and St. Mary's Hall for girls had their beginnings in Faribault, where the same denomination established Seabury Divinity School. The Free Will Baptists opened a seminary at Wasioja in Dodge County. Territorial lawmakers showed their concern for public higher education by providing for a university.

The growing number of schools was not the only evidence that culture was moving westward to the Minnesota frontier. Nearly three thousand of its pioneer citizens subscribed for the *New York Tribune* in 1856. These newcomers of the 1850s found booksellers ready to serve them; in St. Paul William G. Le Duc opened a bookstore in 1851, and three years later William W. Wales set up a similar shop in St. Anthony. Both men also engaged in publishing, Le Duc issuing *Minnesota Year Books* in three successive years. Hundreds of territorial imprints survive to illustrate the Minnesota pioneer's passion for preserving his writings in print. True, many are official in nature, like Governor Ramsey's first message of 1849, which appeared not only in English, but in French and German versions. Sometimes described as the first book published in Minnesota is the earliest number of the Minnesota Historical Society's *Annals*, a pamphlet of twenty-eight pages printed by Goodhue in 1850. Its claim to distinction is based on the fact that, in addition to purely documentary material, it presents an address on French exploration read by Neill before the organization's first annual meeting.

The writings of Minnesotans also began to appear in publications issued elsewhere. Henry H. Sibley contributed accounts of his experiences as a hunter of big game to a well-known national sporting magazine, the *Spirit of the Times,* and Edward Eggleston of *Hoosier Schoolmaster* fame began his career as a professional author while living in Minnesota. Library associations multiplied in number. Both the Mercantile Library Association of St. Paul and the Minneapolis Athenaeum, which proved to be the roots of two great public libraries, began in the 1850s. Active lyceums and debating and literary societies held meetings and arranged public lectures.

Visiting celebrities were not uncommon in frontier Minnesota. Among the literary figures who made their way to the upper Mississippi while steamboats were still the chief means of transportation were Fredrika Bremer, Mrs. Elizabeth Ellet, Laurence Oliphant, Henry David Thoreau, and Anthony Trollope, all of whom eventually published reports of Minnesota's attractions. The great Norwegian violinist, Ole Bull, collaborated with the youthful Adelina Patti in two Minnesota concerts in July, 1856. The crowd that turned out to hear these famed musicians "filled in every nook and corner" of the House of Representatives' hall in the territorial Capitol. Family singing groups, like the Hutchinsons and the Bakers, drew large audiences when they appeared in St. Paul, St. Anthony, and Stillwater. Musical instruments were available through various merchants. In his bookshop, Le Duc sold "all kinds, from a Grand Action Piano to Bass Drums." In 1856 melodeons priced at from forty-five to three hundred dollars were advertised in St. Paul. A growing number of local musicians organized bands, quartets, and similar amateur groups. Dan Emmett of "Dixie" fame lived and worked as a professional musician in the capital city, where his brother Lafayette was a prominent pioneer jurist.

Landscape artists made pictorial records of local scenes. Among those living on the Minnesota frontier in the 1850s were James McC. Boal, Holmes Andrews, and Edwin Whitefield. Moving panoramas of the upper Mississippi, like that painted by Henry Lewis, familiarized Europeans with the Minnesota scene, and doubtless encouraged

THE BALDWIN SCHOOL, organized by Neill, was dedicated in December, 1853. *Engraving based on a daguerreotype by Whitney.*

HARRIET BISHOP of Vermont went west in 1847 to establish a school in Minnesota.

114

WILLIAM G. LE DUC, who opened St. Paul's first bookstore in 1851, had a partner named Daniel Rohrer when this daguerreotype was taken two years later. In addition to books, they sold stationery, musical instruments, and fishing rods.

INGERSOLL HALL, built in 1860 on Bridge Square, St. Paul, was used for plays, concerts, and other types of entertainment. Ole Bull played there in 1869. *Photograph by Illingworth.*

some to emigrate and settle in the Midwest. When a Chicago artist, Thomas C. Healy, traveled to St. Paul in 1857 to paint a likeness of Minnesota's governor, at least one local merchant took advantage of his presence to order portraits of his wife and son. Le Duc displayed some of the engravings issued by the American Art-Union and advertised for subscribers, each of whom was promised a large engraving of an American painting and a chance to win an original oil in one of the union's lotteries.

By the close of the 1850s, Minnesota life was gaining in sophistication as it lost some of its frontier flavor, both culturally and socially. For the protection of life and property, in 1859 the citizens of St. Paul could look to sixteen policemen and a fire department of four companies. The city had a hospital established by the Sisters of St. Joseph. Charges ranged from five dollars a week in a ward to eight dollars in a private room for service that included meals and medical attendance and the use of hot and cold baths. Organizations multiplied rapidly among the newcomers of the 1850s. Many Minnesota pioneers belonged to local lodges of fraternal groups like the Masonic Order, the Odd Fellows, and the Sons of Malta. German immigrants founded a Turnverein that met twice a week in St. Paul; the city's printers organized Minnesota's earliest trade union; local physicians formed a medical society; pioneers joined a branch of the Young Men's Christian Association. Special needs were filled by the Pioneer Hook and Ladder Company, the Minnesota Pioneer Guard, and the Oakland Cemetery Association. All gave evidence of the maturing society that greeted a new decade in the recently organized thirty-second state.

QUARTETS and other small musical groups, composed largely of German settlers, were to be found in many Minnesota communities of the 1850s. *Ambrotype probably taken in the 1860s.*

MINNEHAHA FALLS gained wide publicity with the publication in 1855 of Henry Wadsworth Longfellow's *Song of Hiawatha*. Thereafter, this Minnesota scenic attraction was viewed each year by scores of visitors, some of whom made special trips to see it. *Photograph by W. H. Jacoby, 1868.*

THE GREAT WESTERN BAND of St. Paul was organized by a German musician named George Seibert in 1860. By the close of the 1850s Minnesota had attracted enough musical talent to make possible a group like this. Both the band and its leader continued to play a major role in Minnesota musical life throughout several decades. *Photograph by Illingworth, 1860s.*

116

13.

Statehood and Politics

BY 1857 STATEHOOD was of vital concern to Minnesotans. Governor Gorman stressed its advantages in his message to the territorial legislature of that year and expressed the belief that Minnesota's population was sufficiently large to warrant admission to the Union. The question was under consideration in Washington as early as December, 1856, when the territorial delegate, Henry M. Rice, drafted an enabling act for the future state and introduced it in Congress. After Sibley retired to private life in 1853, Rice had been chosen to represent the territory in the nation's capital, and he was re-elected in 1855. Rice and Sibley had long been competitors and rivals both in the Democratic party and in the upper Mississippi fur trade.

The enabling act that Rice drew up favored the strongly Democratic section of eastern Minnesota, particularly in its definition of boundaries. Obviously the territory, which extended westward to the Missouri, was far too large for a state. Rice and his fellow Democrats, many of whom lived in and about St. Paul, St. Anthony, and Stillwater, wanted to divide the territory with a line running north and south, producing a state bounded on the west by the Red and Big Sioux rivers and on the north by Canada. St. Paul would remain the capital. Rice incorporated this plan into the enabling act, which also provided grants of public lands for schools, a state university, government buildings, and roads, and called for a constitutional convention and a special census. In somewhat revised form, Congress passed the bill and it was approved on February 26, 1857.

While statehood was brewing for Minnesota under the watchful eye of its hardworking delegate in Washington, a new political force—the Republican party—was gaining strength both in the nation and in the frontier territory. The overwhelming Democratic victory in the presidential election of 1852 dealt the old Whig party a blow from which it never recovered. Its failure to take a strong stand on the slavery issue was the chief cause of its decline. Out of this situation evolved the Republican party,

117

which was firmly opposed to the extension of slavery. In Minnesota the party originated in a mass meeting of about two hundred citizens at St. Anthony in the last days of March, 1855. A former Whig, ex-Governor Ramsey, became the territorial leader of the new political organization. Its growth was rapid in the two years that elapsed before Minnesota was ready to take the steps necessary for statehood.

The Republicans were most numerous in the new counties of southern Minnesota and the Minnesota Valley—the area opened to settlement by the treaties of 1851. The party's efforts to give that section a leading position in the future state resulted in a boundary plan quite different from that advocated by Rice and the Democrats. The Republicans favored an east-west division of the territory, making several proposals for lines that would extend westward to the Missouri from the vicinities of such modern communities as Anoka, St. Cloud, and Little Falls. Since a state with these boundaries would be best served by a seat of government in the agricultural Minnesota Valley, the Republicans advanced a plan for making St. Peter the capital. Party leaders implemented the scheme by introducing in the territorial legislature of 1857 a bill for the removal of the capital from St. Paul to St. Peter, and Republican strength was sufficient to carry the measure in both houses.

Then events took an unusual and somewhat comic turn. The bill, which still needed the governor's signature, disappeared, and at the same time Joe Rolette, a Democratic member of the Council from Pembina, was missed in his accustomed haunts. Efforts

ST. PETER was so sure of becoming the seat of Minnesota government that a local townsite company donated land and in 1857 erected a pretentious frame building, planned to accommodate the constitutional convention and early sessions of the legislature. The structure, shown in the center of this photograph taken in 1868, became the Nicollet County Courthouse in 1859.

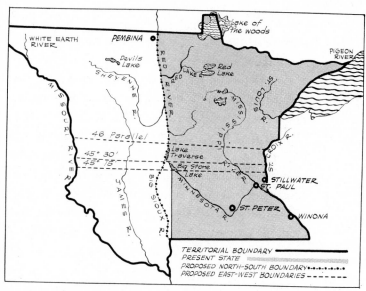

STATE BOUNDARIES proposed for Minnesota in 1857

JOE ROLETTE, a Democratic member of the legislature from Pembina, promoted his party's cause by disappearing with the capital removal bill of 1857. This picturesque fur trader added color to the legislative sessions of the 1850s by attending in modified voyageur garb, which he wore also when he posed for the pastel portrait reproduced at the left.

to locate him and the disputed document proved futile. Not until midnight of March 7, just as the legislature adjourned, did he reappear, bringing the bill with him. A copy had been signed by the governor in Rolette's absence, but the courts decided that it had not been properly passed. In the meantime, overly eager promoters provided St. Peter with a building that could be used as a capitol. But St. Paul remained the seat of government and, fortunately for Minnesota's future, the north-south line became its permanent western boundary.

Although the Republicans lost the legislative battle over boundaries and the location of the capital, they again showed their strength and their growing vitality in the constitutional convention which convened in St. Paul on July 13, 1857. The Democrats, fully aware that their foe was formidable, made every effort to gain control of the convention by electing a larger number of delegates than the Republicans. But of the 114 men who gathered in St. Paul to write a constitution for the future state, 59 were Republicans and only 55 were Democrats. When the convention opened in the House chamber of the territorial Capitol, political rivalry came to the surface as leaders of both parties jumped to the platform and attempted to call the assembly to order by outshouting one another. The violent disagreement reached a climax when the convention split, the Republicans continuing their sessions in the hall of the House of Representatives and the Democrats holding their meetings in the Council chamber.

Weeks passed, and each group wrote its own version of a state constitution. Finally, however, the rivals began to realize that unless they could agree, Minnesota's admission to the Union would be delayed. They named a compromise committee, consisting of five members from each group, who were instructed to resolve the crisis by combining the two documents. Noisy quarrels marked by physical violence marred the sessions of this small and supposedly dignified body before its members produced a constitution which, on August 28, was accepted by both conventions. Even then, each faction demanded its own copy before the delegates would consent to sign the document. Hurriedly produced by weary scribes working by lamplight, the copies vary in some slight details. Thus Minnesota actually has two constitutions. Both manuscripts are among the state archives.

The people of Minnesota approved the new Constitution at the polls on October 13. At the same time, they elected state officials and judges, members of the state legislature, and three congressmen to represent them in Washington. In this contest, the Democrats were victorious. Heading the party's ticket, Sibley defeated Ramsey in the race for the governorship, and the legislature showed a Democratic majority. As specified in the Constitution, the legislators assembled in St. Paul for their first session on December 2. The same document directed, however, that the governor and other state officials could not take office until after the state was admitted by Congress, and that all territorial officers should continue to serve until "superseded by the authority of the state." Thus Minnesota was in an ambiguous situation in the months that passed before Congress accepted its Constitution and admitted it to the Union, since during this period territorial officials ruled in St. Paul while a state legislature that lacked a state held sessions and made laws for a commonwealth that was not yet born.

Whether the measures passed between December 2, 1857, and March 25, 1858, were legal and valid was open to serious doubt. Nevertheless, the lawmakers plunged ahead. In accordance with one of their own legislative acts, they met in joint session on December 19 to elect Minnesota's United States senators. Two ardent Democrats, Rice and James Shields, were named, the first to serve for six years and the second for two. When Congress convened in January, these men were in Washington with William W. Phelps, James M. Cavanaugh, and George L. Becker, the three representatives elected earlier. Anxious and uncomfortable months elapsed before the Minnesota admission act became law, allowing them to take their seats in Congress. Among the matters questioned and discussed at length before the bill received approval was Minnesota's right to three representatives. The special census authorized by the enabling act was taken late in 1857; it revealed a population of 150,037, which would justify only one representative. Congress, however, consented to accept two, and to resolve the problem the three who had been elected tossed a coin. Becker lost and returned to St. Paul.

THE CONSTITUTIONAL CONVENTIONS were held in the House and Council chambers of Minnesota's first Capitol, at Tenth and Wabasha streets, St. Paul. The building was used from 1854 to 1881, when it burned. *Photograph by Whitney, taken before 1872.*

WILLIS A. GORMAN, the first Democrat to serve as governor of Minnesota, played a leading role in his party's section of the constitutional conventions of 1857. *Photograph by Whitney, taken during the Civil War.*

THE REPUBLICAN VERSION of the Minnesota Constitution opens with a neatly written preamble and bill of rights, contrasting sharply with the much-revised Democratic version. In the final result, however, Democratic influence is more evident than Republican. *Courtesy Minnesota State Archives Commission, St. Paul.*

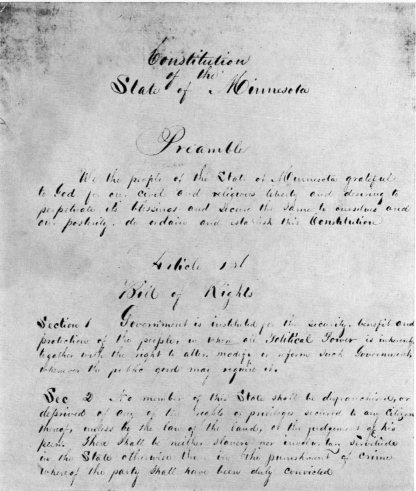

121

Chiefly responsible for the long delay in admitting Minnesota was an attempt to take Kansas into the Union with a proslavery constitution. Although this question, which involved the balance of power between North and South, was not easily settled, a compromise eventually paved the way for passage of the Minnesota bill on May 11, 1858. Then, and only then, were Rice and Shields sworn in and seated in the Senate. Two days later Phelps and Cavanaugh presented their credentials, and after some debate over objections that they had been elected before Minnesota was admitted, they finally were seated more than a week later.

At home in Minnesota it took somewhat longer for the state government to supplant the territorial regime. The mere matter of sending news from Washington to so remote a place as St. Paul involved a lapse of days. Not until the morning of May 13 did St. Paulites learn that they were living in a state capital. An extra issued by the *Pioneer and Democrat* and a handbill printed in the office of the *Minnesotian* announced the "glorious news," which reached Prairie du Chien from Washington by telegraph and then was carried upriver by the steamboat "Milwaukee." A "rumor of admission" spread about Winona after the boat docked there on the evening of May 12, but a definite an-

BRING OUT THE BIG GUN

GLORIOUS NEWS !!

MINNESOTA A STATE !!!

100 GUNS FIRED AT WINONA:

MINNESOTA'S ADMISSION to statehood after six months of weary waiting was greeted with enthusiasm by newspaper editors throughout the commonwealth. These headlines announced the news to readers of the *Winona Times* on May 15, 1858.

122

HENRY M. RICE, Democratic leader, represented Minnesota in Washington from 1853 to 1863, first as territorial delegate and then as United States senator. His likeness is in Statuary Hall of the national Capitol. *Oil by George P. A. Healy, painted in Washington, 1861.*

JAMES SHIELDS was named Minnesota's second senator by the legislature of 1858. Like Rice, Shields was a Democrat. Since he drew the short term, he served only two years. Earlier he had represented Illinois in the United States Senate, and later he served in the same body from Missouri. *Photograph by Brady, probably about 1860.*

SENATOR MORTON S. WILKINSON (left) and Governor Ramsey won Republican victories in 1859 which marked a turning point in Minnesota's political history. *Photograph by Brady, probably about 1860; courtesy National Archives.*

nouncement that "Minnesota has at last been admitted into the Union" as the thirty-second state came only after the message reached St. Paul. Finally, on May 24, the state's executive and judicial officers, who had been elected six months earlier, assembled in the governor's room of the Capitol and took their oaths of office. After the legislature met and heard Governor Sibley's message on June 3, the state government was at long last in full operation.

The Minnesota Democratic regime of 1858 was not destined to remain long in power. In March, 1859, Morton S. Wilkinson, the first of a long line of Republican senators from Minnesota, succeeded Shields. Except for a brief interim appointment at the turn of the century, after 1859 Minnesota sent only Republicans to the upper house in Washington until 1923, when Henrik Shipstead won his seat on the Farmer-Labor ticket. In the state house, too, Republicans soon succeeded Democrats. Governor Sibley served only one term, and Ramsey returned to the governor's chair as the result of an overwhelming Republican victory in 1859. Contributing substantially to this triumph was Ramsey's running mate, Ignatius Donnelly, who became Minnesota's first Republican lieutenant governor. Together the two men made a campaign tour of more than two thousand miles in a "private conveyance," in the course of which each delivered more than sixty speeches. Nationally, also, Minnesota swung into the antislavery Republican column, giving Lincoln 22,000 votes as against 12,000 for Douglas in the election of 1860. In part, at least, Lincoln's success in the state may be attributed to a strong local campaign which brought William H. Seward and Charles Francis Adams to Minnesota to speak on behalf of the Republican candidate. By 1860 the party that was to dominate Minnesota politics for more than half a century was established in a position of leadership.

PART II

A Century of Statehood

1858
1958

14.

The New State and the Civil War

WHEN THE NATION faced the Civil War in April, 1861, Minnesota was the first of of all the states to tender troops for the defense of the Union. Only three years earlier its admission had been long delayed over the very issue from which the conflict stemmed. In the intervening years, Minnesota had taken a decisive stand on that problem by allying itself politically with the antislavery Republican party. Quite by chance, its first Republican governor, Alexander Ramsey, was in Washington on state business on Sunday, April 14, when news of the attack on Fort Sumter spread through the city. Promptly, he went to the office of the secretary of war to offer a thousand men for national defense, and the offer was transmitted to President Lincoln the same morning. Thus began the new state's four-year participation in the Civil War.

Within twenty-four hours the president called for seventy-five thousand volunteers from state militia units, notifying Governor Ramsey that Minnesota's quota would be one regiment of infantry. He relayed the message to St. Paul, where state officials issued an order calling for ten companies ready for service. Volunteers, many of whom had received some military training with local guard units, responded from various localities. Members of the Minnesota Pioneer Guard of St. Paul assembled in the local armory on the evening of April 15 and voted to enlist as a group, which became Company A of the First Minnesota Volunteer Infantry. Units from such communities as Hastings, Red Wing, Winona, Faribault, and St. Anthony took similar action. Before April came to an end, the ten required companies had assembled at Fort Snelling, where 950 members of the First Minnesota were mustered into their country's service. Governor Ramsey was on hand to announce the regiment's field officers, headed by ex-Governor Gorman as colonel. His experience in the Mexican War and as major general of the state militia made him an excellent choice. Neill became the regiment's chaplain.

When the First was mustered in, no uniforms were available, but the state gave each man a blanket, a flannel shirt, and a pair of socks. Arms, consisting largely of Spring-

OFFICERS of the First Minnesota Volunteer Infantry posed in front of the commandant's house before leaving Fort Snelling for the war front in June, 1861. *Photograph by Upton.*

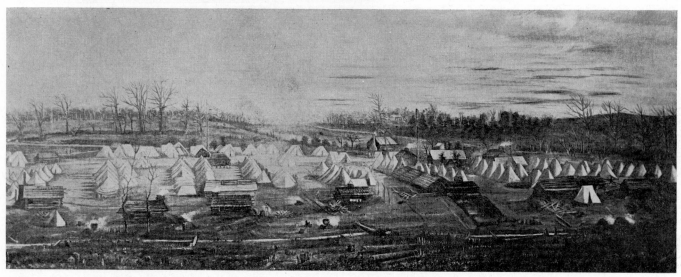

AT CAMP STONE, between Poolesville and Edward's Ferry, Maryland, the First Minnesota was quartered during much of the winter of 1861–62. There officers and men lived in comparative comfort and enjoyed plentiful rations. *Oil by Lillie Z. Hoblit, 1896.*

IN THE BATTLE OF FAIR OAKS, Virginia, from May 30 to June 3, 1862, early in the Peninsular campaign, the First Minnesota fought under General George B. McClellan. This photograph by Brady shows part of the regiment on the battlefield after the engagement.

THE CHARGE OF THE FIRST MINNESOTA at Gettysburg on July 2, 1863, under Colonel William Colvill resulted in the loss of 215 dead and wounded out of a total of 262 participating officers and men, but it did much to make the battle a victory for the Union forces. The painting of this dramatic and decisive action reproduced above was part of Paul Philippoteaux' huge circular panorama of the battle, which was displayed in a specially constructed building in St. Paul for some years following 1886.

field rifles and rifles with sword bayonets, came from the state arsenal or from the equipment used earlier by local militia companies. The ladies of St. Paul and Winona presented the regiment with handsome flags. Before the men left Fort Snelling, each had been issued a uniform consisting of black trousers, a black slouch hat, and a red flannel shirt. Thus strikingly attired, these pioneers so suddenly turned soldiers left Fort Snelling on two steamboats at dawn on June 22. After stopping at St. Paul to march through streets thronged with cheering spectators, they proceeded downstream to La Crosse and Prairie du Chien, where they boarded trains en route to Washington.

Having enlisted to give support to the Union cause, the men were eager for active duty. They did not have long to wait, for on July 21 at Bull Run they received their "baptism of blood and fire." In the months and years that followed, names like Fair Oaks, Savage's Station, Antietam, Fredericksburg, Chancellorsville, and finally Gettysburg took on new and dramatic significance for members of the Minnesota regiment. At Gettysburg, while engaged in a charge that did much to turn the tide of battle toward a Union victory, the First suffered what has been described as the "heaviest loss known" in the annals of modern warfare. Its record is typical of Minnesota's role in the nation's struggle for survival. Before the Confederate surrender in 1865, ten additional volunteer infantry regiments were organized in Minnesota. The state also prepared for active duty and sent to the front two companies of sharpshooters, four cavalry units, a regiment of heavy artillery, and three batteries of light artillery. Some twenty-four thousand Minnesotans served in the Union Army—an impressive number, representing fourteen per cent of the state's total population in 1860.

Not a few of Minnesota's military leaders emerged from the conflict with distinguished records. Four were brevetted major generals and fifteen brigadier generals. After serving as colonel of the First Minnesota for five months, Gorman was promoted to the rank of brigadier general and placed in command of a brigade. His successor, Napoleon J. T. Dana, became a major general. William Colvill was the colonel who led the regiment in its heroic charge at Gettysburg. William G. Le Duc's notable service in the quartermaster department was rewarded by the brevet rank of brigadier general. Among Minnesotans who attained prominence after leaving military service were Colonel Stephen Miller, General Lucius F. Hubbard, and Colonel William R. Marshall, all of whom were elected governors of the state; Chaplain John Ireland of the Fifth Minnesota, who became Catholic archbishop of St. Paul; and General C. C. Andrews, who served as United States minister to Sweden and Norway.

Both men and women who remained on the home front worked for the Union cause and the soldiers' welfare. Unique among Minnesota women was Jane Grey Swisshelm

HANS MATTSON, who founded the Swedish colony of Vasa in 1853, was captain of a company composed largely of Swedish immigrants. He later became colonel of the Third Minnesota. *Photograph by Whitney.*

FATHER JOHN IRELAND was chaplain of the Fifth Minnesota in 1862, when this picture was taken. Like other Civil War chaplains, he did not wear a special uniform. *Courtesy St. Paul Seminary.*

of St. Cloud, editor and publisher of a newspaper known first as the *Visiter* and later as the *Democrat*. In the columns of her paper and from the lecture platform, she actively supported the abolition of slavery long before 1861. Her stand precipitated a crisis as early as 1858, when proslavery Democratic political leaders of the community broke into the office of the *Visiter*, destroyed the press, and threw the type into the Mississippi. Undaunted, Mrs. Swisshelm reopened her office and continued her attacks in a paper that soon appeared under a new name. This crusading abolitionist left St. Cloud in 1863 to become a nurse in a military hospital near Washington.

Like their sisters in other parts of the nation, the women of Minnesota organized a branch of the United States Sanitary Commission to furnish "articles of necessity and comfort not provided by the government" for soldiers who were hospitalized. To raise money for that purpose, early in January, 1865, the women of St. Paul arranged a "Sanitary Fair" marked by all the features of similar fairs in the East. When it opened in Mozart Hall on January 9, there "was a jam" on hand to patronize the art gallery, the fish ponds, and the refreshment stands, and to buy chances on two swords and a piano, which were raffled. The receipts from the event, which closed five days later with a "grand sanitary hop," reached the astounding total of $13,496. One St. Paul woman who labored through those five busy days complained: "I'm nearly dead, ache from the crown of my head to the soles of my feet." Nevertheless, she jubilantly pronounced the fair a "tremendous success."

The year that opened with the St. Paul Sanitary Fair was marked by the end of the war and the home-coming of Minnesota's boys in blue. Some had returned to civilian

THE MEN IN UNIFORM shown above are Otis E. Fowler, aged eighteen, a private in Company K, Seventh Minnesota; Patrick Carel, who wore this picturesque private's uniform after enlisting in Company H, First Minnesota Heavy Artillery, in 1865; and Harry Fifield, drum major and principal musician of Company C, First Minnesota, who displays the white trefoil of the Second Corps, to which his regiment was attached. *Photographs by Whitney.*

WILLIAM G. LE DUC, who had operated a bookstore in St. Paul, was chief quartermaster with General Joseph Hooker's command when this picture of the latter's staff was taken late in 1863 at his winter quarters in the Lookout Valley near Chattanooga. Le Duc is fourth from the right and Hooker is sixth.

THE STEAMBOAT "CHATTANOOGA" was reconditioned under Le Duc's direction to carry supplies via the Tennessee River to Union forces in and near Chattanooga. This photograph, taken by Sweeny in November, 1863, shows the boat unloading forage at Kelly's Ferry, six miles west of the Tennessee city. The supplies doubtless were intended for General Hooker, who captured near-by Lookout Mountain on November 24 in a strategic Union victory.

132

life earlier, among them members of the First Minnesota who were ordered back to Minnesota in February, 1864. The heroes of Gettysburg went by rail to La Crosse and then traveled northward by sleigh on the frozen Mississippi, stopping at towns along the way for welcoming festivities. They were quartered at Fort Snelling until April 29, when they were mustered out. A substantial number re-enlisted, including Colonel Colvill, who assumed leadership of the First Minnesota Heavy Artillery in February, 1865. Not many months were to pass, however, before the veterans of the First and other Minnesota regiments turned to the peaceful pursuits involved in building a new commonwealth.

JANE GREY SWISSHELM of St. Cloud, an ardent abolitionist as early as 1858, filled the columns of her newspaper with articles denouncing slavery. *Photograph by Whitney, about 1860.*

THE ST. PAUL SANITARY FAIR of 1865 raised money for the support of groups like this soldiers' aid society, which packed luxuries for shipment to military hospitals. *Engraving by Thomas Nast, in Frank F. Goodrich,* The Tribute Book (*New York, 1865*).

133

15.

The Sioux War

IN THE SUMMER OF 1862, when thousands of Minnesotans were engaged on the battlefields of the South, the state became involved in a conflict of its own. It was a frontier war with the Sioux, who had been moved onto reservations in the Minnesota Valley after the treaties of 1851. In that restricted area, the nomadic Indians were unhappy, looking with nostalgic longing on the land, now dotted with towns and farms, where once they had been free to roam and hunt. A crop failure in 1861 that left these red men on the verge of starvation, a long delay in distributing their annuity payments, and the appointment of a new agent who showed no understanding of their problems added to their discontent and helped precipitate the crisis of 1862. Important, too, was the Indians' belief that the white man, weakened by another war, would be unable to defend his settlements on the frontier. This belief encouraged a small party of Sioux to kill five settlers at Acton in Meeker County on August 17. After that Chiefs Little Crow and Little Six, or Shakopee, and their followers decided that the time to strike had come.

The excited Indians acted promptly. Early the next morning a large war party attacked the Redwood, or Lower Sioux, Agency, burning buildings, killing the local traders, and looting their stores. At the same time, small groups of Sioux raided farms and crossroads settlements in the vicinity, firing houses and barns, killing the men, and making prisoners of the women and children. The area of fighting expanded rapidly, reaching such remote points as Lake Shetek and Big Stone Lake in a matter of days. The few soldiers at Fort Ridgely, who were expected to defend the frontier, soon realized that their force was inadequate, and sent an appeal for aid to Governor Ramsey. Fortunately, re-enforcements arrived before August 20, when the Sioux under Little Crow attacked the fort. Although they were repulsed by artillery fire, the Indians gathered additional forces and staged a second attack two days later. This time the result was decisive; after losing a hundred men, the Sioux retreated.

134

CHIEF LITTLE CROW of the Kaposia band of Lower Sioux was the principal Indian leader in the Minnesota outbreak of 1862. *Photograph by A. Z. Shindler, 1858; courtesy Bureau of American Ethnology, Smithsonian Institution.*

It had been the red men's hope that by capturing the fort, they could gain control of the entire Minnesota Valley. For a similar reason, they fell upon New Ulm, a substantial German settlement some fifteen miles east of Fort Ridgely. After a preliminary attack on August 19, the Indians returned on August 23 with a greatly enlarged force. The resulting battle, according to Folwell, was "no trivial affair, but an heroic defense of a beleaguered town against a much superior force of infuriated savages." Nearly two hundred buildings went up in flames before the Indians, realizing that they could not take the town, departed. After the battle, the defenders abandoned New Ulm, moving all the inhabitants to Mankato.

During the first few days of the uprising, frightened settlers by the thousands fled from their homes, taking with them little more than the clothes they wore. Refugees took to the roads leading eastward in their frantic efforts to reach Fort Ridgely or larger settlements like St. Cloud, Minneapolis, St. Paul, and even Winona. Some two hundred and fifty took refuge at Fort Ridgely before the attack of August 20. A week after the outbreak began, twenty-three counties in an area two hundred miles long and about fifty miles wide were practically depopulated. Some of those who fled left the state, never to return.

As soon as news of the outbreak reached Governor Ramsey, he began organizing a special force to subdue the Indians. He not only issued a call for volunteers, but obtained from President Lincoln permission to draw into the Minnesota conflict some of the troops already enlisted for Civil War service. With a commission as colonel, Sibley was placed in command of the emergency force on August 19, and the very next day he was moving up the Minnesota by steamboat at the head of four companies of volunteers. He paused for a few days at St. Peter to collect his forces, and by the time he moved on he had a following of fourteen hundred men. In the meantime, the frontier war continued with battles and skirmishes at Henderson, Forest City, Hutchinson, and other points. At Birch Coulee, on September 2 and 3, a detachment under Major Joseph R. Brown was attacked and suffered heavy losses. Not until September 23 did a decisive victory by Sibley's forces at Wood Lake put an end to active hostilities.

Sibley's next concern was for the prisoners held at Red Iron's village on the south bank of the Minnesota River near the mouth of the Chippewa. To this spot, which later was known as Camp Release, the colonel marched with his staff and an escort of troops on the afternoon of September 26. There, encircled by the lodges of the Indians, 269 white and mixed-blood captives, many of them women and children, were turned over to the victors. Sibley had successfully accomplished two objectives of his campaign — the military defeat of the Sioux and the release of their captives.

Although the hostile Sioux scattered over the plains to the west following their defeat at Wood Lake, it was not long before they began to surrender in large groups rather than starve on the open prairie. They posed a new and serious problem for Sibley as the cry of "Death to the murderous Sioux" rang throughout Minnesota. To try them, he set up a military commission of five officers. After beginning proceedings at

FORT RIDGELY was twice attacked in the first week of the outbreak. Although the Sioux succeeded in burning a log barn during the second battle, they were repulsed with heavy losses. *Oil by James McGrew, who participated in the defense of the fort.*

IN THE BATTLE OF NEW ULM on August 23, 1862, about 250 citizen-soldiers, led by Charles E. Flandrau, held the city against double that number of Indians. Twenty-six defenders died and nearly two hundred buildings burned before the Sioux were repulsed. *Oil by Anton Gág, 1893, in the Minnesota Capitol.*

THE BATTLE OF BIRCH COULEE followed a surprise attack on a detachment sent out from Fort Ridgely to bury victims of the massacre. About a hundred horses killed early in the conflict were used as a barricade. Before re-enforcements arrived on the second day of the battle, thirteen men had been killed and forty-four wounded. *From a circular panorama of the Sioux War by Gág, Christian Heller, and Alexander Schwendinger, all of New Ulm, 1893.*

REFUGEES by the thousands fled before the marauding red men. Some encamped on the prairie and many hid for days in swamps and thickets while attempting to reach safety at forts or settlements. *Stereograph taken in 1862.*

Camp Release, they moved to the Redwood Agency, where by late October Sibley's volunteer soldiers and two thousand Indian prisoners of war were encamped. At sessions held from October 25 to November 5, the trial commission disposed of 392 cases, sentencing 307 Indians to death and 16 to imprisonment. The condemned men were sent to a crude prison at South Bend near Mankato, while some sixteen hundred uncondemned prisoners — men, women, and children — were marched off to Fort Snelling. After reaching the post on November 13, they were sent to a wretched camp on the bottom land of the Minnesota River, where they passed the winter.

When the commission had completed the trials, the names of the condemned Indians were sent to President Lincoln. All, it was firmly believed, "had been guilty of voluntary participation in murders and massacres" and should be treated as murderers. Lincoln, however, took a more balanced view of the matter. In his own words, he was "anxious to not act with so much clemency as to encourage another outbreak on the one hand, nor with so much severity as to be real cruelty on the other." He therefore asked for a complete record of the trials and had it carefully examined and sifted by two impartial persons. They were instructed to determine who among the condemned prisoners had been "proven guilty of violating females," and who "were proven to have participated in *massacres*, as distinguished from participation in *battles*." The examiners found only two of the former class, but they concluded that the latter group "numbered forty, and included the two convicted of female violation." Since the sentence of one of this group was commuted on the recommendation of the trial commission, Lincoln ordered that the remaining thirty-nine Indians and half-breeds be executed in punishment for crimes committed during the outbreak. The importance which the president attached to his order may be judged from the fact that he himself penned it with the names of the men sentenced to be hanged and personally forwarded the list to Sibley.

Lincoln's order was carried out at Mankato on December 26, 1862. One of the Indians designated by the president received a respite before that date; thus thirty-eight men were hanged in what has been branded "America's greatest mass execution." On December 27, Sibley sent the president a telegram saying that the guilty Indians and half-breeds had been executed and "Everything went off quietly."

The prisoners remaining at South Bend and Fort Snelling presented another major problem. It was generally felt that all Sioux must be permanently expelled from Minnesota. Finally, in May, 1863, those at Fort Snelling were removed to a reservation at Crow Creek in the Missouri Valley, where they endured three years of dire distress. These Sioux, who came to be known as the Santee, were eventually transferred to a better location near the mouth of the Niobrara River in Nebraska. The men first imprisoned at South Bend spent three years in military barracks near Davenport, Iowa, before being pardoned by the president and allowed to join their families in Nebraska.

Hostilities, however, were not yet over. Most of the red men who surrendered in 1862 were members of the bands of Lower Sioux; the war against the remnants of this group and the Upper Sioux continued. It was feared that Minnesota's frontier communities would be completely abandoned unless the settlers received some assurance of protection against Indian attack. Hastily constructed forts manned by military companies gave hundreds of pioneer Minnesotans a sense of security during the winter of 1862–63 and the summer that followed. Crude posts, often built of logs, were established after the battle of New Ulm in a chain stretching southward from that town to the Iowa border. With troops stationed at South Bend, Madelia, Garden City, Winnebago City, and Blue Earth City, the settlers of the Blue Earth Valley felt that they were being guarded against future attack. A post at Sauk Centre helped restore confidence in an area where there was fear not only of the Sioux but of a possible attack from the north by the Chippewa under Chief Hole-in-the-Day.

Typical of the military units engaged in frontier defense was Company E of the Eighth Minnesota Volunteer Infantry. The regiment was being organized for Civil War service when the Indian outbreak began, and some of its units were promptly detached for frontier duty. Company E, composed largely of farmers from Wright County, was sent first to Monticello; later in 1862, it went to Fort Ripley; it was on duty at the

CAPTIVES held by the Sioux at Red Iron's village were freed on September 26, after General Sibley and his staff "proceeded unmounted but in stately fashion" into what was known thereafter as Camp Release. Many of the whites and mixed-bloods liberated at this time by Sibley's forces were women and children. *From Gág, Heller, and Schwendinger's panorama.*

140

HENRY H. SIBLEY was selected by Governor Ramsey to organize a volunteer force to subdue the Indians. Originally commissioned as a colonel, he rose to the brevet rank of major general by 1865. He not only defeated the Indians, but obtained the release of their captives, supervised the trial and punishment of their leaders, and led an expedition against the Sioux still at large in Dakota in 1863. *Oil portrait by James Fairman; courtesy Sibley House Association.*

Chippewa agency near the mouth of the Crow Wing when annuities were paid in December; and in the spring it was transferred to Paynesville. At some of these places the men built stockades and sod forts. As late as 1864, the Eighth Minnesota went west into Dakota with an expedition against the Sioux, and before the Civil War ended the regiment was ordered south, where it participated in some of the final battles of that conflict.

In command of the forces engaged in the campaign against the Sioux after 1862 was General John Pope of the United States Army. He concentrated some thirty-three hundred men at Camp Pope, near the junction of the Minnesota and Redwood rivers, in June, 1863. Sibley marched westward from Camp Pope with his expedition of that year. General Alfred Sully, a former colonel of the First Minnesota, led other military groups into Dakota in the summers of 1863, 1864, and 1865, searching for hostile Sioux as far west as the Yellowstone River. The frontier was considered unsafe for settlers as long as any of the Indians who participated in the attacks of 1862 were at large; hence military forces searched out every little group that might be roaming the prairies. Some serious battles, marked by heavy losses on both sides, resulted.

Although the story of the expeditions of 1863–65 cannot be followed here, some mention should be made of the fate of two Sioux leaders who were among the Indians

THE CONDEMNED SIOUX were confined in a prison near Mankato after being sentenced. *From* Harper's New Monthly Magazine, *June, 1863.*

IN THIS LOG HOUSE at the Redwood Agency, members of the military commission tried the Sioux involved in the massacre. The house had belonged to François La Bathe, a trader who was killed on the first day of the outbreak. *From* Harper's New Monthly Magazine, *June, 1863.*

pursued by the troops. Both Little Crow and Little Six, the chief instigators of the outbreak, succeeded in escaping after the battle of Wood Lake. Little Crow met an "ignoble end" on July 3, 1863, when he was shot by two deer hunters who failed to recognize him. More than a month passed before the Sioux chief was identified by his son, who was with him at the time of the shooting but succeeded in escaping. Little Six was one of a group of Sioux who crossed the border and took refuge in the Red River country, much to the embarrassment of the Canadian government. Eager to be rid of their unwelcome guests, some Canadians gave Little Six and a companion enough liquor to drink themselves into unconsciousness. In that condition, the Indians were transported across the border and delivered into the hands of Major Edwin A. C. Hatch, who with his battalion of volunteers was stationed at Pembina. Later at Fort Snelling, Little Six was tried and executed. Thus died the last of the leaders of the Indian uprising that racked the Minnesota countryside in 1862.

UNCONDEMNED SIOUX PRISONERS passed the winter of 1862–63 in a camp on the Minnesota River below Fort Snelling. There, in a fenced enclosure, they pitched their tipis and lived on government supplies. *Photograph by Upton, 1862.*

PRESIDENT LINCOLN'S ORDER for the execution of thirty-nine Sioux, written on executive mansion stationery on December 6, 1862, was acquired after the president's death by one of his secretaries, Edward D. Neill. With some other Lincoln papers, he presented the three-page manuscript to the Minnesota Historical Society in 1868. The first and last pages are reproduced herewith.

Executive Mansion,

Washington; December 6ᵗʰ, 1862.

Brigadier General H. H. Sibley
St. Paul
Minnesota.
Ordered that of the Indians
and Half. breeds sentenced to be hanged by the Military
Commission, composed of Colonel Crooks, Lt. Colonel Marshall, Captain Grant, Captain Bailey and Lieutenant Olin, and
lately sitting in Minnesota, you cause to be executed on
Friday the nineteenth day of December, instant, the following
named, towit

"Te- he- hda- ne- chu." No 2. by the record.
"Tazoo" alias "Plan- doo- ta." No 4. by the record.
"Wy- a- tah- to- wah" No 5 by the record.
"Hin- han- shoon- ko- yag." No 6 by the record
"May- za- bom- a- du" No 10. by the record.
"Wah- pay- du- ta." No 11. by the record
"Wa- he- hua." No 12. by the record.
"Sna- ma- ni." No 14. by the record.
"Ta- te- mi- na." No 15. by the record
"Rda- in- yan- kna." No 19. by the record
"Do- wan- sa." No 22. by the record.
"Ha- pan." No 24. by the record.

"Hda- hin- hday." No 373. by the record.
"O- ya- tay- a- koo." No 377. by the record.
"May- hoo- way- wa." No 382. by the record.
"Wa- kin- yan- na." No 383 by the record
" The other condemned prisoners you will hold sub. ject to further orders, taking care that they neither
escape, nor, subjected to any unlawful violences.
Abraham Lincoln, President of the United States.

143

THE EXECUTION of the guilty Sioux at Mankato on December 26, 1862, was reported and illustrated in newspapers and magazines throughout the nation, and was pictured in lithographs and panoramas. Although martial law was declared in the Mankato area and troops were on hand to prevent violence, a great crowd witnessed the spectacle. *From John Stevens' panorama of the massacre, painted in the late 1860s.*

144

THE SAUK CENTRE STOCKADE was typical of posts erected after 1862 to ensure protection for settlers. Company B of the Eighth Minnesota was there in the summer of 1863. *Oil painted in 1864; courtesy Sauk Centre Public Library.*

LITTLE SIX was a doleful prisoner at Fort Snelling for a year and a half before he was executed on November 11, 1865. *Photograph by Whitney.*

AT CAMP POPE on the Minnesota River, the military force involved in the campaign of 1863 assembled. *From A. P. Connolly,* The Minnesota Massacre *(Chicago, 1896).*

16.

The Minnesota
Indians after 1862

MINNESOTA'S INDIAN POPULATION was radically reduced after the Sioux Outbreak of 1862. A Congressional act of February 16, 1863, expelled from the state both the Sioux and the Winnebago—about ten thousand red men. This left fewer than seven thousand Chippewa living in Minnesota's northern forest area.

The behavior of some of these woodland Indians had not been altogether above reproach during the uprising of 1862. Although long hostile to the Sioux, the warlike and pugnacious Chippewa Chief Hole-in-the-Day made an effort to join his old enemies in their revolt against advancing civilization. He managed to gather a following among members of his own Gull Lake band and the Pillagers of Leech Lake, but he could not induce them to attack the Chippewa agency at Gull Lake. They indulged in enough plundering, however, to alarm the settlers in the area of Fort Ripley, who turned to the post for protection. A council of other Chippewa chiefs and a special agent settled the difficulties and greatly reduced Hole-in-the-Day's prestige. Eventually, in 1868, he was murdered by his own men.

Toward the close of the century, when the nation was involved in the conflict with Spain, a group of Leech Lake Pillagers once more demonstrated hostility toward the white man. Aroused by frauds in the disposition of dead timber on their lands and by attempts to arrest some of their people for illegal liquor sales, some thirty-five Indians led by a member of the Pillager band named Bugonaygeshig battled with a detachment of the Third United States Infantry from Fort Snelling at Sugar Point on the east shore of Leech Lake. The engagement, on October 5, 1898, lasted three and a half hours and resulted in the killing of six men, including Major Melville C. Wilkinson, the officer in command, and the wounding of ten others.

Following the battle, fear of a general uprising spread through northern Minnesota, and troops were rushed into the area. Included were about three hundred officers and men from Fort Snelling and two batteries of the Minnesota National Guard. It took a

146

visit from the commissioner of Indian affairs and the persuasion of an influential Catholic missionary, Father Aloysius Hermanutz, to pacify the Chippewa. Their encounter with United States troops was among the last battles in the long history of Indian hostility against the whites.

In the interval between the forays of 1862 and 1898, the Mississippi Chippewa were concentrated on a large reservation in northern Minnesota. Parts of this area remain today as the extensive White Earth, Red Lake, and Leech Lake reservations. Far smaller areas occupied by Chippewa groups are located in the vicinities of Nett and Mille Lacs lakes, at Lake Vermilion near Tower, at Grand Portage, and at Fond du Lac near Duluth. The Lake Superior bands occupy the two latter reserves.

The leader in a movement to improve conditions among the reservation Chippewa and to obtain favorable treaties for them was Bishop Henry B. Whipple of the Episcopal church. It had a mission station among the Gull Lake Chippewa as early as 1852, and Whipple went there immediately after he became bishop of Minnesota in 1859. His concern for the physical as well as the spiritual welfare of the red men caused one historian to name him Minnesota's "Apostle to the Indians." Whipple's work on their behalf earned him the red men's respect and confidence.

Active also among the Chippewa were the Catholics. The pioneer missionary priest, Father Francis Pierz, founded a congregation at Grand Portage in 1838. Twenty years

CHIEF HOLE-IN-THE-DAY was unsuccessful in his attempt to lead a Chippewa revolt against the whites in 1862. *Daguerreotype taken about 1855.*

later he established a mission at Red Lake, and he continued to visit it until 1866, long after he moved his center of operations to Crow Wing. A log chapel built at Red Lake in 1879 was replaced by a church dedicated in 1893, and in 1889 a school was opened there for the Indians. Father Aloysius, a Benedictine from St. John's Abbey at Collegeville, went to White Earth in 1878 with two nuns of the same order, who established a school. The Benedictines have ever since served the Chippewa, both as spiritual leaders and as teachers.

Although many of them have adopted the white man's way of life, the Chippewa have continued some of their ancient customs, practices, and occupations. The teachings of their ancestors are handed down by the Medewiwin or grand medicine society, which holds meetings in lodges constructed on a traditional pattern. Although many reservation Chippewa do some farming and logging, they still make maple sugar, tan hides, do beadwork, make moccasins, and harvest wild rice. Family groups migrate to the sugar bush in the spring, tap the trees, collect sap, and boil it down to make syrup or sugar. Harvesting wild rice has become a profitable activity since the white man has acquired a taste for this wilderness delicacy. The Minnesota crop averages 500,000 pounds a year, and in 1956, a bumper yield produced 1,200,000 pounds of finished rice, and provided an income of about $1,200,000 to the harvesters, most of whom were Chippewa Indians. Another industry that supports many a Chippewa family is commercial fishing on Red Lake. Members of the Red Lake Fisheries Association, a co-operative group run by Indians at Redby, take over a million pounds of fish from Red Lake each season, and some fishermen earn as much as two thousand dollars a year.

Still living within Minnesota's borders, in addition to the Chippewa, are small groups of Sioux — descendants of Indians who remained behind when their tribesmen were expelled or who returned to their old haunts after memories of the outbreak were somewhat dimmed by time. Most of those who stayed were Christians living at Mendota under Sibley's protection or near such other communities as Faribault, Red Wing, and Shakopee. Although these faithful red men lost both their lands and their possessions as a result of the uprising, many received farms in new locations after 1884, when Congress passed the first act providing for their welfare. Among them was Good Thunder, whose farm near Morton in the Birch Coulee area became the center of a settlement of the Lower Sioux. An Episcopal mission established there in 1887 and long headed by a native pastor, the Reverend Henry St. Clair, continues as St. Cornelia's Church at Morton.

Four additional Sioux communities are still to be found in Minnesota — near Granite Falls in Yellow Medicine County, at Prairie Island near Red Wing in Goodhue County, at Prior Lake near Shakopee in Scott County, and at Pipestone in the county of that name. The latter, which centers about the famed red stone quarry, is both the oldest and the most interesting. As a reservation of 648 acres, it was set aside in a treaty with the Yankton Sioux in 1858, and except for a small grant for a railroad right of way, it remains intact today. The Pipestone National Monument, established in 1937, em-

148

BUGONAYGESHIG, who is pictured at the left, led an uprising of Bear Island Pillagers against the white man at Leech Lake in 1898. With a small group of warriors, he defeated a detachment of regular army troops from Fort Snelling on October 5. *Photograph taken in 1897; courtesy National Archives.*

TWO UNITS of the Minnesota National Guard, under the command of Major Elias D. Libbey, went to the Leech Lake area to help suppress the uprising of 1898. While on active duty at Cass and Leech lakes and at Brainerd, the guardsmen drilled in the field to music furnished by their own band.

THIS TYPICAL RESERVATION VILLAGE of log houses on Leech Lake was photographed about 1890.

braces about a fifth of the reservation, including the quarry. The right to obtain pipe-stone is reserved exclusively to Indians, and members of any tribe have free access to the quarry.

Somewhat surprising is the fact that Minnesota's Indian population, far from dwindling, has shown substantial growth since 1862. True, the Sioux are few in number; only 656 were enumerated in the census of 1950. In the same year, however, 12,533 Indians, largely Chippewa, were counted in the state. When this figure is compared with 8,761 in 1920, the rate of increase is evident. Mixed-bloods and red men living outside reservations doubtless were not always included in the census as Indians, since a reliable source estimated the state's native population at 18,000 in 1949. The red men's desire to leave the reservations, especially after attaining full citizenship rights in 1924, is reflected in the fact that by 1950 Indians were living in forty-three of the state's eighty-seven counties. There is evidence that after 1950 several thousand took up residence in Hennepin and Ramsey counties, largely in the Twin Cities, where employment opportunities were available to them. Ninety-five years after the expulsion of the Sioux, Minnesota's Indians seem to be not only more numerous than they were before the tragedy of 1862, but as widely distributed throughout the state.

LARGE LOTS OF SUPPLIES like those pictured above, which were received at Grand Portage in 1887, were sent to reservation Indians under the terms of various treaties with the Chippewa. *Courtesy St. Louis County Historical Society.*

THE CATHOLIC CHURCH at Grand Portage was built in 1863 and still stands in 1958. In the cemetery near by, the miniature houses that mark pagan Chippewa graves are seen beside crosses. *Photograph taken in 1885; courtesy St. Louis County Historical Society.*

THE CATHOLIC MISSION SCHOOL at White Earth provided instruction for both Indian and white children. *Photograph taken about 1900; courtesy Convent of St. Benedict, St. Joseph.*

EARLY EPISCOPAL MISSIONARIES to the Chippewa included the Reverend James Lloyd Breck, who was photographed about 1860 with two native preachers, Isaac Manitowab in the center and Enmegahbowh, or John Johnson, at the left.

BISHOP HENRY B. WHIPPLE worked for the general welfare of all Minnesota Indians and established missions for both Sioux and Chippewa. *Photograph by George Prince, 1898; courtesy National Archives.*

ST. CORNELIA'S EPISCOPAL CHURCH at Morton, built in 1891, was attended largely by loyal Sioux of 1862 or their descendants. Members of the congregation and their pastor, the Reverend St. Clair, posed for this picture about 1900.

THE MEDEWIWIN or grand medicine society of the Chippewa holds meetings and conducts some ceremonies in lodges of bent poles. *Photographed at Elbow Lake on the White Earth Reservation by Frances Densmore, 1909; courtesy Bureau of Ethnology, Smithsonian Institution.*

CHIPPEWA WOMEN continue to smoke and tan buckskin for making moccasins and other typical articles of clothing. *Photograph taken about 1910.*

BIRCH-BARK CANOES were still constructed by some reservation Chippewa in the early years of the present century. They used traditional methods long familiar to their ancestors. *Photograph taken about 1910.*

WILD RICE is harvested in flat-bottomed boats or canoes, each occupied by two Indians. One poles the craft slowly through the water while the other uses sticks to bend the stalks and knock the rice grains into the boat. The harvest takes place between August 15 and September 15.

THIS CHIPPEWA FISHERMAN, photographed as he raised his nets with the day's catch, is typical of several hundred Indians who engage in commercial fishing on Red Lake. *Photograph, 1950; courtesy* Minneapolis Sunday Tribune.

THE PIPESTONE RESERVATION of the Sioux centers about the quarry where for generations Indians of all tribes obtained the red stone from which they carved pipes. *Photograph taken about 1900.*

155

17.

New People
on the Land

FOLLOWING MINNESOTA'S ADMISSION to the Union, people from many parts of the globe arrived to establish homes on the lands once occupied by the Sioux and the Chippewa. The migration gained momentum after railroad companies joined the state in extending what a mid-century ballad called a "general invitation to the people of the world." It met with an enthusiastic response, especially among farmers who were needed to cultivate vacant government and railroad lands and provide traffic and freight for the network of rails built after 1862. In wagons, covered and uncovered, on foot, by boat, and eventually by rail, newcomers flocked to the upper Mississippi, passing through St. Paul and Minneapolis on their way to the promised land where farms were to be had for little more than the asking. The great wave of European migration that began to move into Minnesota after statehood continued to swell until the early years of the twentieth century. In the later decades of this period, many of the landseekers boarded transcontinental trains at St. Paul bound for unoccupied areas beyond Minnesota. Census figures prove, however, that the North Star State kept within its boundaries a generous share of the emigrants who left the Old World in the half century after 1860.

Among those who established homes in Minnesota before 1880 were 267,676 natives of foreign lands. Throughout the remainder of the century, the movement of people into Minnesota continued to accelerate until 1910, when 543,595 foreign-born were to be found among the state's 2,075,708 inhabitants. A slow decline in the number from other lands followed this high point. In 1920 Minnesotans of foreign birth numbered 486,795, and by 1957 the state could count only 170,291 naturalized citizens over twenty-one years of age out of an estimated total population of 3,300,000. Federal restrictions on immigration account in large part for the reduction.

The immigrants who trooped westward into Minnesota in the late decades of the nineteenth century came largely from northern Europe — Germany, Sweden, Norway,

156

Denmark, and Great Britain, especially Ireland. By 1900 there were 117,000 Germans and more than 236,000 Scandinavians in the state. They settled largely on farms — the Germans in the Minnesota Valley and the St. Cloud area of Stearns County; the Norwegians in the southeastern counties of the state and the Red River Valley; the Swedes in the triangle between the St. Croix and the Mississippi and in Kandiyohi and Meeker counties; the Irish in Swift and other western counties and in the cities, especially the state's capital.

With the approach of a new century, large contingents of people from eastern and southern Europe began to seek homes in Minnesota. Forerunners of these groups were the Czechs who settled in Le Sueur and McLeod counties before 1880. Among the latecomers who added substantially to Minnesota's population after 1900 were Finns, Poles, Hungarians, Yugoslavs, Rumanians, Lithuanians, Russians, Italians, and Greeks. Many of these new immigrants were laborers rather than farmers, and they settled largely in the Arrowhead country of northeastern Minnesota, where they found work in the mines and the forests.

Cheap land, cheap transportation, a healthful climate with a temperature range much like that of the homeland, absence of class distinctions, and political and religious freedom were among the advantages that lured the multitudes from northern Europe to the center of the North American continent in the late nineteenth century. The virtues of the New Canaan were described not only in pamphlets published in English, German,

THE WESTWARD TREK to Minnesota began when emigrants, like these Germans who embarked at Hamburg, boarded a ship at a European port. *From* Harper's Weekly, *November 7, 1874.*

HORDES OF EMIGRANTS often jammed the steerage on Atlantic liners.
Photograph by Underwood and Underwood, New York, 1906; courtesy Library of Congress, Washington, D.C.

Swedish, and other languages for distribution by the thousands at home and abroad, but by agents who carried personal messages to prospective emigrants in Europe. Typical was Hans Mattson, a pioneer from Sweden who was secretary of the state board of immigration from 1867 to 1870. In addition to his official duties, he acted as land agent for the St. Paul and Pacific Railroad, going abroad for his company in 1871, despite the fact that he had been elected Minnesota's secretary of state. Largely as a result of Mattson's enthusiastic advertising campaign, Meeker and Kandiyohi counties became centers of Swedish settlement. He and others were able to offer farms on a railroad for from three to ten dollars an acre, depending upon quality and accessibility. Like other land-grant roads with vast tracts to sell, the St. Paul and Pacific looked to the proceeds to help finance construction, pay operating expenses, and ensure future business along its line.

158

IMMIGRANTS had their first glimpse of the New World from Ellis Island. *Photograph by Underwood and Underwood, 1912; courtesy Library of Congress.*

WAGON TRAINS were often used by westward-bound immigrants before through rail connections were available. This party of about a hundred Swedes set out from Boston in 1851. *From* Gleason's Pictorial, *July 26, 1851; courtesy Library of Congress.*

THIS "EMIGRANT SLEEPER" on the Northern Pacific afforded accommodations much like the steerage of an ocean liner, with wooden bunks and a cookstove. *From Harper's Weekly, September 13, 1886.*

RAILROAD WAITING ROOMS were crowded with immigrants from many lands in the 1870s. *From Frank Leslie's Illlustrated Newspaper, August 18, 1887.*

Agents like Mattson who worked abroad often sold transportation to prospective emigrants, issuing tickets for the entire journey from the point of embarkation to Minnesota to avoid any possible mistake in destination. The railroads did everything they could to make it easy and inexpensive for recent arrivals from lands across the Atlantic to reach the West. Among the inducements offered to Minnesota-bound immigrants were reduced rates both on ships and railways. Some Minnesota roads allowed settlers to deduct travel expenses from the price of any lands they purchased; others transported newcomers with their families, stock, and personal property at half the regular rates. As a result of such advantageous arrangements, an emigrating Norwegian could make the entire journey from his homeland to Chicago for less than fifty dollars in the late 1860s.

Europeans who took advantage of these low rates continued to receive special treatment after reaching Minnesota. Upon arrival at a railroad division point, a newcomer found accommodations awaiting him at an immigrants' reception house, where he was given shelter and a chance to buy food and even clothing at cost while he looked for land in the vicinity. The St. Paul and Pacific erected such reception centers at Litchfield, Benson, Morris, Willmar, and Breckenridge; the Lake Superior and Mississippi operated several between St. Paul and Duluth; and the Northern Pacific established them at Duluth, Brainerd, and Glyndon. All were "fitted up with cooking-stoves, washing conveniences, and beds." The largest, at Duluth, was equipped to accommodate a hundred people.

Once established on his own farm, the settler could erect a house for about two hundred dollars, according to a booklet issued in 1872 by the Northern Pacific. It included plans for a residence measuring sixteen by twenty feet, with living room, bedroom, and pantry on the ground floor and an "attic large enough for good sleeping-accommodations." In 1871 settlers also could purchase from a Brainerd manufacturer "ready-made houses" costing from one to five hundred dollars — frontier forerunners of modern prefabricated dwellings.

The excitement of the great movement of people who migrated to Minnesota between 1860 and 1910, or filtered through it to the regions beyond, did much to color the state's history in that restless era. Characteristic is the scene described by a traveler who boarded a transcontinental express at the St. Paul Union Depot on a May afternoon in 1886. There in addition to "Long lines of cars standing on the tracks, locomotives hissing and tooting, bells clanging; luggage trucks lumbering back and forth," he saw "anxious mothers, crying children; soldiers; emigrants — Germans, Scandinavians, Scotch, English, and Irish . . . broad-brim-hatted, flannel-shirted, weather-beaten frontiersmen, their bedding and luggage corded up in canvas or buffalo-robes and slung over their shoulders; a 'dude' of the British species, with a whole paraphernalia of guns, fishing-rods, hat-boxes, etc.," all westward bound. Such scenes, typical of the trek from Europe to mid-continental America, were attractive to both artists and photographers. Reproduced herewith are some pictorial records of that dramatic migration into the American West.

LAND OFFICES like this one at Alexandria sold government tracts to settlers under the Homestead Act of 1862. Any citizen or newcomer who had his first papers could obtain title to a quarter section by paying the land-office fee and living on or cultivating the tract for a period of five years. *Photograph by N. J. Trenham, 1876.*

IMMIGRANTS often arrived at the St. Paul Union Depot in colorful native costumes. Among them were these Alsatians who were photographed in 1902 while en route to new homes in northern Minnesota.

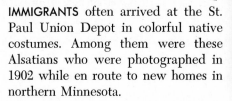

A COLONISTS' RECEPTION HOUSE at Glyndon, operated by the Northern Pacific, offered settlers free accommodations and information about available lands. *Photograph by F. J. Haynes, 1876; courtesy J. E. Haynes, Bozeman, Montana.*

SETTLERS bound for points beyond Minnesota's boundaries filtered through St. Paul by the thousands. Among them were members of this colony of Dunkers, who traveled westward on a special train over the Great Northern Railroad and stopped in the yards of the St. Paul Union Depot while en route from Indiana to the Red River Valley of North Dakota in March, 1894. *Courtesy State Historical Society of North Dakota, Bismarck.*

COVERED WAGON TRAINS moved settlers westward to lands beyond the end of steel in the late nineteenth century. These prairie schooners were photographed in Manitoba. *Courtesy Public Archives of Canada.*

18.

Farmers in a
Changing Economy

THE FARMERS who made up the bulk of Minnesota's population in the year of the state's birth lived simple lives, using comparatively primitive methods to work the land and maintain self-sufficient establishments. For any products their families did not consume, the pioneers found a local market at stores or mills in frontier settlements. As new arrivals from other states and from Europe occupied lands farther and farther from the early centers of population, however, and railroads gave them readier access to markets, farming lost much of its simplicity. In the course of a century, the farmers' means of livelihood was transformed into a highly complicated business, dependent upon machinery and scientific methods, organized on a commercial basis, and serving a world market.

The first radical change in Minnesota agriculture centered about wheat. As wars at home and abroad, better transportation, and improved milling methods provided an expanding market for the grain in the 1860s, Minnesotans responded by concentrating on this cereal crop. They turned to newly introduced machinery, which reduced production costs and made large-scale farming profitable, especially on the cheap prairie lands of western Minnesota. As early as the 1870s, farming became big business in the state as some of its citizens organized bonanza farms of a thousand acres and more, usually in the Red River Valley, where they raised wheat only. By the middle of the decade, wheat had become king in Minnesota, and two-thirds of the state's tilled land was devoted to the crop. During this era, Minnesota attained a reputation as "the bread basket of the world."

Between 1870 and 1880 the Minnesota wheat crop nearly doubled, increasing from eighteen to more than thirty-four million bushels. The growth reflected in these figures was not, however, uninterrupted. Most spectacular of the setbacks to wheat production was the plague of Rocky Mountain locusts, or grasshoppers, which descended upon the state each summer from 1873 to 1877. In some areas the insects devoured every

164

growing plant, and in one year they are said to have destroyed fields that would have yielded more than two million bushels of wheat. To combat the pests, the state and some counties offered bounties for locusts captured by the bushel, sometimes making grasshoppers a "more profitable crop than wheat." Another formidable enemy encountered by pioneer wheat farmers was stem rust. Although adequate records of the disease were not kept until about 1917, reports indicate that rust was a destructive pest as early as 1878. Such reverses notwithstanding, Minnesota led the nation in wheat production until after the turn of the century. Nevertheless, the late decades of the 1800s were marked by the beginning of diversified farming in the southeastern section of the state. The change is usually associated with the census year 1880, when cattle and hog raising, butter and cheese making, and the production of corn and small grains were reported—a pattern that eventually spread throughout the state.

The Minnesota Dairymen's Association was organized in 1878. By the middle of the next decade the industry had attained substantial proportions, with some sixty creameries and more than forty cheese factories operating in the state. The co-operative movement, which has characterized the entire growth of Minnesota dairying, began in the late 1880s, and in 1890 a group of Danish farmers applied the plan at Clark's Grove. By 1909 more than five hundred Minnesota creameries were organized on this system. Co-operative marketing, established on a state-wide basis by the Land O'Lakes creameries after 1921, also did much to stimulate the growth of dairying. Minnesota now ranks first among the states in the production of butter. Other dairy products distributed in quantities running into millions of pounds or gallons include cheese, ice cream, and milk. Farm co-operatives of many types had become important in the state's economy by the mid-twentieth century; in 1956 Minnesota led the nation with a total of 1,321 such organizations. Of these, 933 were marketing co-ops and 388 were farm supply associations. Together they did a combined business of more than $636,700,000.

As wheat profits declined, Minnesota farmers turned to new crops as well as to dairying. To supplement wheat, they planted corn, oats, barley, flax, alfalfa, and fruit trees. By 1910 oats had replaced wheat as the state's most profitable cash crop, and in 1940 corn, in turn, took the lead over oats, accounting by 1956 for more than eight per cent of the total cash farm receipts in Minnesota. After World War II, soybeans, a crop in-

THE FRAME HOUSE in which this Lincoln County farm family lived in the 1880s represented a great advance over the sod hut used earlier by frontier settlers in southwestern Minnesota.

THE COUNTRY KITCHEN was a center of family activity in most farm homes. Note the fiddle and almanacs hanging on the rear wall of this cluttered room.

troduced commercially in the 1930s, steadily increased in importance, and since 1951 it has ranked second to corn. Among other outstanding products, particularly in the Red River Valley, are sugar beets and potatoes. The changing status of Minnesota crops is well reflected in agricultural statistics for 1957, when the state placed second among the forty-eight commonwealths in oats production; third in corn, soybeans, and flax; eighth in sugar beets; and seventeenth in wheat.

Livestock, too, has become a lucrative factor in Minnesota's economy, accounting for three-fourths of the farmers' income from agriculture in 1956. From some two hundred thousand cattle on the state's farms in 1867, the figure soared to a million in 1885, and to four times that amount in 1957. Hogs, which numbered a hundred thousand in 1860, totaled more than three million in 1957. Thousands of Minnesota farmers also raise chickens and turkeys. Chickens and eggs were of sufficient importance in 1874 to warrant the organization of a State Poultry Association, and both products retain leading roles in the agricultural economy of the 1950s. The state usually ranks second or third in the production of eggs. Turkey raising has developed largely since 1929, but Minnesota today ranks second among the states, with a record of more than nine million birds in 1956.

Agricultural organizations appeared in Minnesota in the territorial era, when county groups began to arrange fairs for the display of local products. An association of this type, which was active as early as 1854, was incorporated by the legislature as the Minnesota State Agricultural Society in 1860. Under its auspices fairs were held at such points as Fort Snelling, Red Wing, Winona, Rochester, and Owatonna, as well as in St. Paul and Minneapolis. The rivalry of the latter cities for a time threatened the very existence of Minnesota's state fair, and some years, notably 1878, saw competing exhibitions, one in each community. The problem was resolved, however, in 1885, when the legislature accepted from Ramsey County a gift of two hundred acres on the

166

outskirts of St. Paul but within easy reach of both cities. The site, first used in September, 1885, became the permanent location of Minnesota's annual state fair. Originally devoted largely to agricultural and livestock exhibits of interest chiefly to farmers, the exposition has become far more varied. By 1915, mechanical, educational, and art displays had been added, and various types of entertainment were being staged in the grandstand and on the midway. With the expansion of the grounds and the erection of substantial buildings, space has become available for the scores of diversified displays and other attractions which drew well over a million people to the Minnesota State Fair of 1958.

Many types of rural organizations have flourished in Minnesota. Some, like the Patrons of Husbandry, or the Grange, and the Farmers' Alliance, had political aspirations. Others were composed of individuals interested in the advancement of dairying, poultry raising, stockbreeding, woolgrowing, and horticulture. The 4-H club movement reached Minnesota in 1912. Among the chief aims of this rural youth organization is the improvement of livestock, which receives substantial encouragement at Junior Livestock shows held annually at South St. Paul since 1918. Much of the credit for the popularity of 4-H clubs in Minnesota goes to Theodore A. Erickson, their state leader for more than a quarter of a century. Before he retired in 1940, the Minnesota clubs had nearly fifty thousand members.

"Dad" Erickson, as he was generally known, is only one of numerous leaders who have contributed substantially to agricultural progress in the course of a century. Peter Gideon, experimenting in his orchard near Excelsior in the 1850s, developed the Wealthy apple and other varieties of fruits that will survive severe northern winters. Wendelin Grimm, a German immigrant who began to farm in Carver County in 1857, worked with alfalfa until he succeeded in producing the hardiest of all known varieties. William G. Le Duc, who served as commissioner of agriculture under President Hayes, encouraged the cultivation of sorghum. Theophilus L. Haecker, who was associated with the dairy school of the University of Minnesota from 1891 to 1918, devoted his energies to promoting co-operative dairying, and he is considered largely responsible for its success in the state. Also connected with the state university were E. C. Stakman, a plant pathologist who successfully combated stem rust in wheat by developing rust-resistant varieties, and Fred E. Haralson, a horticulturist whose name has been given to an apple that will not only thrive in a cold climate but will keep well in storage.

All evidences of progress notwithstanding, agriculture has not succeeded in retaining its traditional position as the leading producer of revenue among Minnesota occupations. In the mid-twentieth century, industry forged ahead of agriculture and urban population outgrew rural. Twenty-five rural counties showed a loss of population in the years from 1950 to 1956. The number of farms in the state dropped after 1945, and the percentage of land in farms — almost two-thirds of the total area — also decreased slightly. What the future holds for Minnesota's farmers can only be guessed. That they will continue to play an important role in the state's economy can scarcely be doubted.

LUXURIES AND CONVENIENCES were sometimes enjoyed by farm families while living in log cabins. These pioneers of 1890 had both a piano and a sewing machine.

A QUILTING BEE gave the farm women pictured at the right a chance for a rare social gathering. *Courtesy State Historical Society of North Dakota.*

LOG CABINS like this one, built near Lake Itasca by John Korth, once dotted Minnesota's northern cutover areas. *Photograph by Mary G. Logan, about 1902; courtesy John Dobie, St. Paul.*

CLEARING LAND in wooded areas involved both cutting trees and pulling stumps. Horses were used in the latter operation on this Wabasha County farm. *Courtesy Mrs. Gerber.*

A BARN-RAISING sometimes was the occasion for a social get-together in which neighbors helped build the structure and then joined in celebrating its completion. *Photograph taken in Wabasha County, 1910; courtesy Mrs. Gerber.*

BREAKING THE TOUGH SOD of the virgin prairie in areas like the Red River Valley and southwestern Minnesota required the pulling power of two yoke of oxen. *Courtesy Public Archives of Canada.*

STEAM THRESHERS operated by crews of seasonal workers who took the machines from farm to farm during the harvest were available in Minnesota as early as the 1860s. *Photograph taken near Plainview, 1898; courtesy Mrs. Gerber.*

HARVESTING WHEAT on a bonanza farm like that operated after 1876 by Oliver Dalrymple near Casselton, North Dakota, involved hundreds of migratory laborers and dozens of horse-drawn reapers. *From Harper's Weekly, July 30, 1887; courtesy Library of Congress.*

170

GRASSHOPPERS, which destroyed Minnesota crops in the 1870s and 1880s, were captured in nets by settlers who collected bounties on their catch. *From* Frank Leslie's Illustrated Newspaper, *September 1, 1888; courtesy Library of Congress.*

ELEVATORS for the storage of wheat began to dot the Minnesota landscape at shipping points as railroads pushed westward. This one, erected at Moorhead in 1878, pioneered in serving the bonanza farms of the Red River Valley. *Photograph by Ole E. Flaten, 1879; courtesy Clay County Historical Society, Moorhead.*

AT LOCAL CREAMERIES, Minnesota farmers sold surplus milk and cream, thus supplementing incomes once largely dependent on field crops. The co-operative shown below was organized at Claremont, Dodge County, in 1891. *Photograph taken about 1900; courtesy Dodge County Historical Society, Mantorville.*

MODERN DAIRIES, many of them co-operatives, are equipped with machines which not only fill paper cartons with milk but form and seal them. *Photograph by Frank A. Staffenson, 1957.*

TURKEY RAISING became important in Minnesota after 1930. By 1954 almost two million birds were produced in Kandiyohi, Otter Tail, Becker, Aitkin, and Renville counties, leading centers of the industry in Minnesota. This flock of a thousand birds was raised on a farm operated at Effie in 1932. *Courtesy Richard H. Anderson, Big Fork.*

172

THIS ELABORATE EXHIBIT at the Minnesota State Fair of 1902 included grains, fruits, and vegetables raised in fertile Goodhue County. *Photograph by Elgin R. Shepard.*

CATTLE JUDGING drew a crowd to the grandstand during the State Fair of 1902. After being held in various other localities, the exposition obtained a permanent home in St. Paul in 1885. *Photograph by Shepard.*

CONTOUR FARMING, used to stop erosion in hilly areas, is illustrated in this view of Houston County taken about 1950. *Photograph by Victor Johnson.*

THIS TYPICAL FARM in Goodhue County was photographed from the air in 1950. *Courtesy Agricultural Extension Service, University of Minnesota, St. Paul.*

THRESHING MACHINES that depended on gasoline for power replaced steam equipment in the 1920s. The later use of tractors has greatly reduced the size of the threshing crew required.

19.

Exploiting Natural Resources

THE STATE'S rich soil, its lush forests, its extensive ore beds, its waterways, and the power sites along their courses have played significant roles in Minnesota's economy. The technological revolution that occurred in agriculture during the past hundred years was matched in other industries like mining and lumbering. New sources of supply and scientific forestry practices have transformed the area's forest products industry — a business that once depended almost solely upon white pine. With the impending depletion of its high-grade iron ores and changes in steelmaking methods, the state's mining industry has evolved complex beneficiating equipment to utilize its enormous supplies of low-grade ore and taconite. Thus Minnesota's first century of statehood has seen major changes in the use of its natural resources.

By 1858 some of Minnesota's resources had already been extensively exploited and in one instance almost exhausted. The fur-bearing animals, which were the basis of the area's first big business, had largely disappeared from its woods and streams in the late 1850s, and the great buffalo herds that once roamed its prairies had moved westward into the Dakotas. The fur trade, which had been the backbone of the upper Mississippi Valley's economy, reached its peak in the 1830s and then declined.

Unlike furs, other natural resources have continued to figure prominently in the state's economic progress since 1858. Logging and lumber production, which centered in the St. Croix and Rum River valleys before statehood, shifted northward as the best pine stands of these regions were exhausted and others became available on the headwaters of the Mississippi and in the Arrowhead country. By 1900 the lumbering frontier had shifted to Beltrami, Itasca, St. Louis, and other northern counties, which harbored a gigantic industry conducted by huge companies that sent thousands of men into the woods each winter. During the cutting season, these lumberjacks worked and lived in camps in the forests; in the spring they drove logs on streams that often became choked with timber. Booms, where the logs were sorted, and rafts destined for saw-

LUMBERJACKS, like these photographed in 1890, who spent their winters in camps in the forests, worked at felling trees, removing the branches, and sawing the trunks into logs.

LOGS WERE LOADED onto sleighs drawn by oxen or horses for transportation, over corduroy or iced roads, from the woods to the waterways. *Photograph taken near Cloquet about 1928.*

mills were other features of a large-scale industry that stripped billions of feet of high-grade lumber from Minnesota's forests between 1870 and 1910.

Most of the timber cut during this era was white pine. As the superb stands disappeared from the shores of lakes and streams, the industry moved inland, where less accessible virgin timber still awaited the ax and the saw. By 1890 a network of railroads built by lumbermen to move the logs crisscrossed much of the wooded section of northern Minnesota, and lines and spurs extended into many a remote area. In recent decades trucks have taken over much of the work performed earlier by logging railroads, but in the mid-twentieth century the bulk of the state's primary forest products still moves to market via rail or water. Nevertheless, steel rails had largely disappeared from the remote forests of the north country by 1941.

Gone, too, was the white pine that once gave Minnesota a leading place among logging states. In 1899 it ranked second, with an annual output of more than two billion board feet, ninety-three per cent of which was white pine. These figures marked the peak of production, and the decline that followed was rapid. By 1909 lumber production in the state had decreased by a third, and in 1933 — at its lowest point — the cut totaled only forty-nine million board feet.

Although the state now produces about two hundred million board feet of lumber each year, it does a far more extensive and valuable business in pulpwood, which is processed by eleven mills. Twentieth-century lumbermen have found new sources of supply and new uses for Minnesota's second-growth timber like aspen, jack pine, and poplar, as well as for its spruce and basswood. In addition to paper of varying grades and types, its plants manufacture such items as wallboard, insulating materials, matches, clothespins, barrels, shingles, and similar products. Minnesota customarily ranks first in the production of sash and door frames. The cutting and processing of Christmas trees and wreaths has also become a lucrative business in recent years. In fact, the value of

WANIGANS often served as cook shacks and stores for the men who were engaged in the log drives. *Photograph probably taken in the 1890s.*

A LOG JAM filled the St. Croix River from bank to bank at Taylors Falls on the 1884 drive. *Courtesy Washington County Historical Society, Stillwater.*

AT THIS BOOM NEAR STILLWATER, logs that moved down the St. Croix were sorted according to the distinctive marks used by each lumber company. *Photograph taken in 1872.*

AT RAFTING GROUNDS on Lake St. Croix expert crews assembled logs into gigantic rafts for transportation to mills located farther downstream. *Photograph taken about 1896.*

178

the state's forest products has increased greatly since 1899. In that heyday of white pine, Minnesota's forests yielded a return of some $42,689,000, while the woodland harvest of 1956 had an estimated value of $197,435,000. At mid-century, with forests occupying almost 19,500,000 acres — more than a third of the state's land area — the future of its timber products industry seems promising.

Two-thirds of the nation's annual supply of iron comes from mines in northeastern Minnesota that constitute the state's most spectacular natural resource. Strangely enough, the presence of ore was only vaguely suspected and its extent was completely unknown until long after 1858. The explorations which resulted in the discovery of iron deposits on Minnesota's three great ranges—the Vermilion, the Mesabi, and the Cuyuna—extended over the years from 1865 to 1895.

The earliest mines were located on the Vermilion, northernmost of the ranges. After surveying the area in 1865, a geologist named Henry H. Eames told of finding iron ore,

SEVERAL LARGE SAWMILLS located in Stillwater (right) used some of the logs that were sorted at the St. Croix boom. *Photograph taken about 1875; courtesy Washington County Historical Society.*

PULPWOOD, the most valuable product of Minnesota's forests in the 1950s, is used in huge quantities by this paper mill at Cloquet.

UNDERGROUND methods are used on all three Minnesota ranges. This picture was taken in the Sellers Mine at Hibbing in 1906. *Courtesy Library of Congress.*

but he took little interest in his discovery, for he was seeking gold. His report of the presence of the yellow metal in the area helped to instigate a short-lived gold rush which distracted attention from iron for another decade. Then in 1875 and again in 1880, exploring expeditions searched for iron in the Lake Vermilion area, and the results encouraged eastern investors to buy large blocks of land in the vicinity. Within two years Charlemagne Tower had organized the Minnesota Iron Company, established a town which was named for him, and built a railroad to connect the new community with Two Harbors on Lake Superior. Commercial iron mining in Minnesota began when the first ore was shipped over this line in 1884. The region promptly experienced a boom, and by 1890 almost three hundred companies had been incorporated to operate in the area.

The decade of the 1890s was marked by the discovery of more extensive iron resources on the famed Mesabi Range, southwest of the Vermilion. The finders of these valuable deposits were Leonidas Merritt of Duluth and his six brothers. As timber cruisers, they were familiar with the heavily wooded Mesabi Range, a scarcely perceptible height of land in an area of dividing waters. Although the brothers were convinced that there was iron on the Mesabi, for twenty years they searched in vain. Then, in 1890, a lumber wagon sank into soft, red soil and gave them a clue. When a sample of the rust-colored earth was analyzed, it was found to contain sixty-four per cent pure iron. The ore that the Merritts had long believed to be underground was, much to their surprise, on the surface, ready to load onto cars and ship out. All they needed to exploit the Mountain Iron Mine and other rich deposits soon located in the neighborhood of Vir-

180

THIS BENEFICIATING PLANT, built by the Oliver Mining Company near Coleraine in 1907, was the first in Minnesota to experiment with the processing of the state's low-grade ores.

THE MAHONING MINE near Hibbing on the Mesabi Range, which looked like this in 1899 less than a decade after its discovery, has become part of the Hull-Rust-Mahoning Mine, the largest open-pit operation in the world. *Courtesy Miss Edith L. Beardsley, Hibbing.*

ginia was a railroad. The story of the Duluth, Missabe and Northern Railroad, which the brothers built with financial aid from John D. Rockefeller, and of the loss of their holdings in the panic of 1893, is well known. Vast wealth was needed to develop the rich resources the Merritts discovered. By 1900 the great steel companies of the East controlled the Mesabi mines, which were producing more iron than any others in North America.

A third Minnesota range, the Cuyuna lying southwest of the Mesabi largely in Crow Wing County, was discovered in 1895 by a surveyor named Cuyler Adams. Years passed before this area was developed, and the first ore was not shipped until 1911. The deposits on this range now supply most of the nation's manganese. Both on the Cuyuna and the Vermilion the ore lies in veins and is mined by means of conventional shafts leading to underground tunnels. Although this method is used also on the Mesabi, open-pit mining has been more widely employed there because the ore was originally found near the surface.

By the end of Minnesota's first century of statehood, the rich ores of the Mesabi with over fifty per cent iron content were believed to be nearing exhaustion. In an effort to utilize the large remaining supplies of low-grade ores, the Oliver Mining division of United States Steel constructed the first experimental beneficiating plant in the state on the shore of Trout Lake near Coleraine as early as 1907. A later development is the processing of taconite, devised after decades of experiment by Professor E. W. Davis of the University of Minnesota school of mines. His method, which concentrates the lean iron content of the magnetic taconite found on the eastern Mesabi into pellets containing over sixty per cent of the metal, is the basis for a new industry centering in Minnesota's Arrowhead country. There two companies, which began production in 1952 and 1957, have built plants, shipping facilities, and new towns like Babbitt, Silver Bay, Hoyt Lakes, and Taconite Harbor. Their establishments were among the seventy-eight beneficiating plants operating on the Mesabi and Cuyuna ranges in 1957. Thanks to concentrates and to taconite, it seems likely that iron will continue to play a significant role in Minnesota's economy.

ORE CARS by the hundreds, most of them loaded with red earth bound for the docks at Duluth, appear in this photograph taken in the 1920s in the yards of the Duluth, Missabe and Northern Railroad at Proctor, west of the Lake Superior port.

182

DOCKS like this one owned by the Oliver Mining Company at Duluth, and scores of others both there and at Two Harbors, are specially constructed for loading Great Lakes ore boats. Railroad cars, carrying ore from Minnesota's iron ranges, run on top of the structures to dump their loads down chutes into the holds of waiting boats.

SILVER BAY and the Reserve Mining Company's taconite processing plant have appeared on the north shore of Lake Superior since 1952. *Photograph taken in 1956; courtesy Reserve Mining Company, Duluth.*

Among the state's other natural resources, building stones, sand, and gravel are important. In 1954, for example, Minnesota's sand and stone shipments were valued at about $22,500,000 — more than ten times the figure for 1939. The state ranked third in 1954 in the production of granite, which is quarried in ten counties concentrated in three areas — near St. Cloud and Cold Spring, in the upper Minnesota River Valley from New Ulm to Ortonville, and in the Arrowhead region north of Duluth. The industry began modestly with a single quarry in the St. Cloud area in 1868, and by 1900 the handsome and varicolored granites of the vicinity were much in demand as building materials. Limestone, used in building the oldest structure in the state — the Round Tower at Fort Snelling — is still quarried extensively along the Minnesota and Mississippi rivers. It was obtained near Winona as early as 1854, and the well-known Kasota quarries in Le Sueur County have been in operation since 1868. Granite for the St. Paul Cathedral was cut at Rockville; Kasota stone and St. Cloud and Ortonville granites are used extensively in the Minnesota Capitol; and the state has furnished granite for important structures across the nation from New York to California.

MOST OF THE LIMESTONE that is quarried at Mankato and elsewhere in the state is utilized in crushed form for road building and animal feeds, and in making cement and asphalt roofing.

GRANITE QUARRIES in the St. Cloud-Cold Spring area use complex equipment like this coring machine that cuts cylinders out of the rock. *Courtesy Cold Spring Granite Company, Cold Spring.*

Minnesota's lakes and rivers provide the resources for its fishing industry. About 460 commercial fishermen are licensed each year to operate on Red Lake, Lake Superior, and the Mississippi, and perhaps 45 more work on other waters, including the St. Croix River, Lake of the Woods, and Rainy and Namakan lakes. Among fish caught commercially are lake trout and herring in Lake Superior, carp in the rivers, and walleye and northern pike, tullibees, and whitefish in other lakes. Sturgeon, taken from Lake of the Woods in large numbers in the 1890s, was exploited for its caviar and has almost disappeared; and lake trout, which represented a Lake Superior catch of almost 189,000 pounds as recently as 1954, are rapidly declining in number due to depredations of the sea lamprey. In 1957 only 35,400 pounds of trout were taken. Such setbacks notwithstanding, more than 6,000,000 pounds of fish valued at over $640,000 were caught in Minnesota waters by commercial fishermen in 1957. Mention should be made also of the clamming industry which prospered along Lake Pepin in the first quarter of the twentieth century. Mussel fishermen who operated on the upper Mississippi supplied the raw materials used by two button factories at Winona, and they often obtained pearls of considerable value. The clam beds, however, have almost disappeared, and with them the clammers.

Numerous other resources have figured in Minnesota's economy. The harvesting of wild rice is discussed elsewhere, and the pioneers' interest in ginseng and cranberries has been noted. In 1868, fifty to seventy-five barrels of cranberries were shipped daily during the harvest to eastern markets, where they sold for more than three dollars a bushel. One dealer purchased seventy-five thousand pounds of ginseng in Minnesota in 1865. The demand for the medicinal root has continued, and in 1957 it was worth sixteen dollars a pound. Buffalo bones gathered by settlers on the western plains were shipped into Minneapolis, chiefly between 1884 and 1891, by a firm known as the Northwestern Bone Syndicate, which sold these last remains of the once great herds to manufacturers of bone charcoal at from five to seven dollars a ton. In addition to lumber, some of Minnesota's forests, especially in the Big Woods area, yielded maple sugar. Hennepin County residents made more than two hundred thousand pounds in 1868, when the price was twenty cents a pound. Such resources, however, had only a slight and often temporary effect on Minnesota's economy. They cannot compete in importance with the forests, the iron mines, and the water power which have been essential in the molding of the industrial state.

BUFFALO BONES gathered at Saskatoon, Alberta, for shipment to Minneapolis in 1890 represented the last vestige of an exhausted natural resource once plentiful in Minnesota. *Courtesy Hudson's Bay Company.*

MACKINAW BOATS were commonly used by commercial fishermen on Lake Superior in the 1890s. Those pictured at the right were setting gill nets. *Photograph taken about 1892; courtesy National Archives.*

FISHING BOATS of substantial size, used on Lake Superior in the 1950s, are pictured below after unloading their catch for the day at the Duluth docks. *Courtesy St. Louis County Historical Society.*

186

FISHERMEN like this Lake of the Woods opera-tor of the 1940s dry their nets on wooden reels. *Photograph by John Dobie; courtesy Minne-sota Department of Conservation, St. Paul.*

CLAMMERS who took mussels from the waters of the upper Mississippi and Lake Pepin in the 1890s were seeking both fresh-water pearls and shells. The latter were used by button factories in the area, which did a prosperous business particularly in the first two decades of the twen-tieth century. *Photograph by Edward A. Bromley.*

20.

From Waterways
to Airways

TRANSPORTATION FACILITIES and means of rapid communication were among the most urgent needs of the new state in 1858. Steamboats chugging up the Mississippi and the Red for seven or eight ice-free months each year had provided the first regular transportation between Minnesota and the outside world. In winter, dog sleds, stagecoaches, and an occasional ice train ran somewhat spasmodically over frozen trails and streams. Even when operating on more or less regular schedules, stage lines were a poor substitute for railroads. The cry for the iron horse was not answered until 1862, when ten miles of rails were completed between the capital and St. Anthony by the St. Paul and Pacific road. Minnesota's pioneer locomotive, the "William Crooks," made its initial run over this stretch on July 2, inaugurating a second phase in the state's transportation history.

During the decade that followed, an ever expanding railroad system carried the benefits of year-round communication to communities remote from waterways. More than two hundred miles of steel had been laid at the close of 1865, and by 1873 that figure had multiplied tenfold. The panic of 1873 put a temporary stop to construction, but building was resumed in 1877. When a new decade dawned, Minnesota had more than three thousand miles of track, and its major trunk lines were virtually completed.

By 1880 many of the state's early roads had been absorbed by rival companies salvaged from the panic by two transportation giants — Henry Villard and James J. Hill. Villard completed the Northern Pacific, the first of the northern transcontinental lines, marking his achievement by personally driving home the last spike at Gold Creek, Montana, on August 22, 1883. Some two weeks later, Minnesotans staged elaborate parades and lavish banquets at St. Paul and Minneapolis in honor of the hero who at long last had succeeded in linking their state with the Sea of the West.

Hill had long been active in steamboat freight traffic on both the Mississippi and the Red rivers before organizing a company to buy the bonds of the bankrupt St. Paul and

188

STAGECOACH routes covered some 1,300 miles in Minnesota in the 1860s and 1870s. This stage ran regularly about 1876 between Alexandria and Melrose. *Photograph by Trenham.*

WATER AND RAIL TRAFFIC met at Moorhead in the 1870s, when agricultural implements, lumber, and various other American products were exported to Canada via the Red River. *Photograph by Flaten, 1879; courtesy Clay County Historical Society.*

BARGES carrying coal and petroleum products account for over ninety per cent of the freight that reaches Minnesota via the Mississippi. *Photograph by Kenneth M. Wright Studios, St. Paul.*

THE "WILLIAM CROOKS,"
which is still designated as
No. 1 in the Great Northern's
locomotive roster, is on permanent display in the St.
Paul Union Depot. Hill is
standing on the step in this
photograph taken in 1907.
*Courtesy Great Northern
Railway Company, St. Paul.*

Pacific in 1878. That early Minnesota railroad was soon extended northward across the international boundary under a new name — the St. Paul, Minneapolis, and Manitoba. Then Hill's road began to reach toward the Pacific, and finally in the early days of 1893, as the Great Northern, its transcontinental line was completed to Seattle. But even there, the Empire Builder did not stop. He extended his sphere of influence by acquiring large blocks of Northern Pacific stock when it failed in the panic of 1893, by gaining control of the Chicago, Burlington, and Quincy to give his roads an independent route to Chicago, and by establishing a Pacific steamship line to connect the American Northwest with the Orient.

Although the outlines of Minnesota's railroad pattern were discernible as early as 1880, mileage continued to increase. The Soo Line, built between Minneapolis and Sault Ste. Marie, Michigan, in 1887 by the flour-milling interests, shorter roads constructed to haul iron ore from newly discovered mines to Lake Superior ports after 1884, and the branch and feeder lines of earlier roads doubled the mileage between 1880 and 1900. The climax came in 1920, when the state could claim 9,114 miles of track. Then began a slow decline, as more flexible forms of transportation began to compete with the iron horse. By 1957 the figure had dropped to 8,303. Included in this mileage are three major railroad webs, the largest of which focuses on the Twin Cities and embraces the Great Northern, the Northern Pacific, and the Soo Line. A second pattern, in southern Minnesota, is geared toward Chicago; and a third in the northern and western sections, feeds the port of Duluth.

First among the railroads' competitors were motor vehicles, which ushered in the third phase of Minnesota's transportation history about the turn of the century. A few gasoline-propelled horseless carriages appeared on the streets of Minneapolis as early

190

THE NORTHERN PACIFIC'S TRACKS, extending across Minnesota from Lake Superior, ended near Brainerd in 1871, when the picture at the right was taken by Illingworth.

HENRY VILLARD, builder of the Northern Pacific, was welcomed as a hero in St. Paul on September 3, 1883, after the "golden spike" ceremony marked the completion of his line to the Pacific. *From* Harper's Weekly, *September 15, 1883.*

HILL'S ROAD was pushed westward across the Great Plains in 1887 by crews that often completed eight miles of line in a single day. While laying nearly seven hundred miles of track in North Dakota and Montana, the men lived in the three-story dormitory cars pictured at the right. *Courtesy Great Northern Railway Company.*

THE GREAT NORTHERN, completed in 1893, became Minnesota's second transcontinental road after the last spike was driven near Scenic, Washington, on January 3. *Courtesy Great Northern Railway Company.*

AN AUTOMOBILE, a bicycle, and several other forms of transportation were involved in this Minneapolis traffic jam of 1905 at Sixth and Nicollet.

as 1895; a St. Paul dentist had a commercially manufactured Winton in 1899; and in 1900 J. George Smith drove his electric Waverly in the Minnesota capital. In the Mill City a motorist was arrested in 1902 for exceeding the speed limit, which was ten miles an hour. By the time the state began to issue metal license plates in 1907, Minnesotans owned about five hundred automobiles. Figures have soared ever since. Licensed motor vehicles in 1920 totaled more than three hundred thousand, over seven hundred thousand in 1930, and almost a million and a half in 1957.

Out of increased motor traffic arose a need for more and better roads. To supervise their construction, the Minnesota highway commission was established in 1906, and in 1921 it was replaced by the state highway department. Its first commissioner, Charles M. Babcock, planned the state's trunk highway system. Before leaving his post in 1933, Babcock supervised the building of more than six thousand miles of trunk highways. Many of them were hard-surfaced roads; concrete, for example, was first used in Minnesota in 1913, when an experimental strip was laid. Babcock's department recorded

A FLEET OF EIGHTEEN BUSSES, including the twelve vehicles pictured below, was operated in the Hibbing area in 1918 by the Mesaba Transportation Company, a forerunner of the Greyhound system. *Courtesy Mrs. Andrew G. Anderson, Hibbing.*

MUDDY ROADS, which plagued auto owners in 1927, were improved through the joint efforts of the state highway department and the AAA. *Courtesy Minnesota State Automobile Association, Minneapolis.*

CLOVERLEAF INTERSECTIONS, like this one on Highways 36 and 61, have taken the place of major crossroads on modern highways. *Courtesy Minnesota Highway Department, St. Paul.*

145 miles of paved roads in the state in 1920; ten years later it had 1,434 miles; and in 1954 the figure was 90,000 out of a total of 122,757 miles of highways.

Minnesota's highways are used not only by automobiles but by passenger busses and freight trucks. Two Minnesotans, Carl E. Wickman and Andrew G. Anderson, played pioneering roles in the history of bus transportation, for from a route they established at Hibbing in 1914 grew the national Greyhound system. On the local level, busses provide city transportation. Almost nine hundred, for example, were running in 1956 on the streets of the Twin Cities, where only a few years earlier they replaced the electric streetcars that began to operate in the 1890s. The number of trucks licensed to operate in the state more than doubled between 1936 and 1957, increasing from 114,516 to 241,170. By 1950, when about sixty Minnesota motor carrier systems hauled an estimated 3,600,000 tons of interstate freight, trucking had become big business. Truck lines connect the state's three major cities, as well as smaller centers that are not served by railroads.

194

TWO OPERATORS (above) handled the calls passing through the gas-lighted Minneapolis South Exchange of the Northwestern Telephone Company in the 1890s.

THE FIRST TELEPHONE SWITCHBOARD in Minnesota (left) was installed in the Minneapolis City Hall in 1877.

While motor transportation was showing vigorous growth in Minnesota, the Mississippi, once pushed into the background by the railroads, again became an important traffic route. The work of the Upper Mississippi River Improvement Association, organized in 1902, ultimately resulted in a nine-foot channel. It became a reality in 1940, after the completion of a series of twenty-six locks between Minneapolis and St. Louis. The river has since served as an avenue for an extensive trade in coal, gasoline, oil, grain, and other freight carried largely to, and in smaller quantities from, the upper river in barges. At St. Paul and Minneapolis, this traffic reached a total of 3,180,496 tons in 1957 — almost three times the figure for 1941. Water transportation has attained vast proportions, too, on Lake Superior, where boats carry grain and ore eastward and return loaded with various products, chief among which is coal.

Along with transportation, several forms of word communication made rapid strides after Minnesota became a state. Well established at the dawn of statehood were newspapers, which totaled seventy-five in 1858. They continued to increase rapidly until

195

shortly after the turn of the century, when about seven hundred were appearing regularly. Many have since ceased publication and others have consolidated, resulting in a sharply reduced figure. The loss, however, is more than offset by increased circulation, for swifter production and improved transportation enabled the 425 Minnesota newspapers issued in the spring of 1958 to serve at least twice as many readers as their forebears of 1905. The first telegraph line, built from Chicago via Winona, was opened for business in St. Paul on August 29, 1860, and by the end of the year both St. Anthony and Minneapolis had their own service. The pioneering Northwestern Telegraph Company, which had more than five hundred offices scattered throughout the Northwest before 1871, was absorbed ten years later by Western Union, the largest company of its type in the entire nation.

Following the telegraph was the telephone, which in Minnesota appeared first in Minneapolis. There a crude switchboard made of old sewing machine parts was installed in the City Hall in 1877, and within a few months it was serving eleven customers. St. Paul acquired its first exchange a year later, and the Duluth telephone company was incorporated in 1881. By 1915 some seventeen hundred companies were operating in Minnesota. Consolidation gradually reduced the number to about three hundred in the 1940s, and by 1955, one company, the Northwestern Bell, was responsible for a large proportion of the 849,000 telephones in use in Minnesota. Radio made its bow in 1921 with a station on the campus of the University of Minnesota. It was soon followed by the commercial stations that became WCCO and KSTP and by numerous others, until sixty-one were broadcasting in the state in 1957. Still another method of communication became available to Minnesotans on April 27, 1948, when the state's first television station began operations. Nine years later, in 1957, Minnesota had one educational and nine commercial stations.

Mail deliveries were irregular and undependable when Minnesota became a state in 1858. River packets carried messages as well as passengers and freight to the older settlements along the waterways; couriers who traveled on horseback in summer and by dog sled in winter provided mail service for such remote communities as Pembina; stage drivers tucked sacks filled with letters under the seats of coaches crowded with passengers. With railroad expansion, the new transportation medium took over the mails, which henceforth were far more frequent and regular. Post offices multiplied; rural free delivery, which first penetrated southern Minnesota in 1896, carried mail to hitherto isolated farms and cabins; and parcel post was inaugurated in 1913. By 1956 letters and packages destined for Minnesotans were passing through 5,796 post offices.

The most recent improvement in postal service came in the 1920s, with the arrival of air traffic as the fourth phase of the state's transportation history. Flying exhibitions thrilled state fair visitors as early as 1910, and a venturesome pilot soared over Minneapolis in January, 1913. Then, in 1920, air mail service was authorized between the Twin Cities and Chicago, with planes operating from a wooden hangar on what became Wold-Chamberlain Field in Minneapolis. Disaster, however, plagued the line, which was

196

WINTER MAIL SERVICE for isolated north shore residents of the late nineteenth century was provided by couriers who used dog sleds. *Stereograph taken about 1890; courtesy George Eastman House, Rochester, New York.*

SPLIT ROCK LIGHTHOUSE, built on the north shore of Lake Superior by the United States government in 1910, is the only structure of its kind in Minnesota. Its light, which can be seen for twenty-two miles, warns mariners of dangerous rocks and shallows below.

A MAIL BOAT, the "Siskiwit," operated on Lake Superior during the summer months in the 1890s to serve people living between Duluth and Fort William. *Photograph taken about 1895; courtesy St. Louis County Historical Society.*

THE DETROIT LAKES POST OFFICE of 1900 (left) was typical of such main street establishments throughout Minnesota.

PARCEL POST, inaugurated in 1913 when the picture at the right was taken, was used extensively by St. Paulites during the Christmas season of that year.

soon discontinued. Finally, Northwest Airways, organized by Colonel L. H. Brittin of St. Paul, agreed to reopen the route and inaugurated the new service on October 1, 1926. As Northwest Airlines this organization has continued to expand, making the Twin Cities a center of international air traffic. It still operates from Wold-Chamberlain Field, which it now shares with five other commercial airlines. To and from that terminal, Northwest carried 107 paying passengers in 1927, when it began to transport travelers as well as mail. Thirty years later, in 1957, well over a million passengers used Minnesota's largest airport. Although Wold-Chamberlain is the busiest of the state's airfields, no fewer than 437 others existed within its boundaries at the opening of its centennial year.

Waterways, railways, highways, and airways combine in 1958 with a strategic location near the geographical hub of the continent to make Minnesota a transportation center as well. By providing ever faster and shorter routes to the Orient, railroads and airlines have fulfilled the dreams of explorers who three centuries earlier penetrated this land of dividing waters while searching for the mythical Northwest Passage to the Far East.

THE FIRST AIRPLANE to fly over Minneapolis circled the Hennepin County Courthouse in subzero weather on January 12, 1913. Alexander T. Heine was the pilot.

AIR MAIL SERVICE between the Twin Cities and Chicago, first authorized in 1920, began to operate regularly after Northwest Airways took over the route on October 1, 1926. *Photograph taken in 1929.*

199

PASSENGER SERVICE was added to Northwest's program in 1927. A year later, these patrons boarded one of its planes piloted by Charles W. ("Speed") Holman. *Courtesy Northwest Airlines, St. Paul.*

WOLD-CHAMBERLAIN FIELD had become a huge international airport on the outskirts of the Twin Cities in 1956, when this picture was taken. *Courtesy Northwest Airlines.*

CHARLES A. LINDBERGH, JR., a youthful aviator from Little Falls, made the first solo trans-Atlantic flight in 1927. He and Holman are Minnesota's most famous air transportation heroes.

21.

A Tale
of Three Cities

MINNESOTA'S WATERWAYS, which had provided paths for explorers and guided the course of pioneer settlement, also determined the locations and special characteristics of its three major cities. St. Paul grew up at the head of navigation on the Mississippi; St. Anthony and Minneapolis were founded on opposite banks of that river at a major water-power site; Duluth is situated at the westernmost point on Lake Superior and the Great Lakes.

Well established before Minnesota was admitted to statehood, St. Paul, St. Anthony, and Minneapolis were growing cities by the time the Civil War began. Although it was not platted until 1854, Minneapolis on the west bank of the river at the falls absorbed the older St. Anthony in 1872. By 1880 it had replaced St. Paul as the state's largest community. After the Civil War Minnesota's third large city, Duluth, at the head of Lake Superior, began to show promise of future greatness. Between 1870 and 1955, these urban centers grew, until by the latter year some 1,450,000 people—almost half the state's total population—were concentrated in the three cities and their mushrooming suburbs.

The stretch of unnavigable water below the Falls of St. Anthony was a fundamental factor in the evolution of St. Paul. It was only natural that a city founded where steamboat traffic up the Mississippi was obliged to halt should become a commercial center, and that it should later develop as a transfer point for the railroads which replaced water transportation. After the Civil War, St. Paul became a jobbing center for such commodities as groceries, wool, furs, hides, dry goods, hardware, and drugs. By 1880 manufacturing, too, was becoming important in the Minnesota capital, and it was the state's financial hub, with brokerage firms and insurance companies supplementing its banking facilities. Printed items, sashes, doors, and blinds, clothing, beer, and cigars were among the commodities produced on a large scale by hundreds of St. Paul factories in the 1880s. After 1900 meat packing assumed importance, reflecting the progress of the

201

RIVER AND RAIL transportation met on the St. Paul water front in the middle 1880s. The steamboat is the "J. J. Hill," named for the St. Paul railroad magnate who was interested in both forms of traffic. The Union Depot, which served the city from 1881 until 1920, is in the center.

stockyards opened in 1887 at suburban South St. Paul — a community that climbed to second place among the nation's livestock markets by 1956. Today such varied products as adhesive tapes, electronic computers, calendars, and derricks are manufactured in huge plants, most of which have set up headquarters in St. Paul since 1900.

While its reputation as a commercial and industrial center was growing, St. Paul did not lose sight of the fact that it was also the seat of state government. A gleaming Capitol dome looming above the sky line of the city's business district is a perpetual reminder of its century-old function. The first Capitol, which was destroyed by fire in 1881, was replaced two years later by a brick building on the original Wabasha Street site. It was, however, soon outmoded and outgrown, and within a decade plans were in progress for the imposing structure of white marble which overlooks the city from Capitol Heights. Designed by a distinguished local architect, Cass Gilbert, the exterior was erected between 1896 and 1902, and the interior was ready for a legislative session in January, 1905. The Capitol has become the nucleus for a group of buildings that house the Minnesota Historical Society and provide office space for a rapidly expanding array of state departments.

Minneapolis was characterized in its early years by an industrial growth that depended upon the Falls of St. Anthony for power. At the turn of the century the city was both the world's leading lumber market and America's foremost flour-milling metropolis.

THE BUSINESS AND RESIDENTIAL sections of St. Paul had spread westward along the Mississippi to the High Bridge by the closing decade of the nineteenth century. This panoramic photograph was taken from Cherokee Heights, on the west side of the river.

ST. PAUL'S EARLY MOVIE HOUSES, where "refined vaudeville and photo-plays" could be enjoyed for ten cents, centered about the corner of Seventh and Wabasha streets in 1912. This busy intersection also marked the edge of the city's retail shopping district. *Photograph by Kenneth M. Wright Studios.*

203

MINNESOTA'S SECOND CAPITOL served the state from 1883 to 1906. The modest red brick structure occupied a square block between Wabasha and Cedar at Tenth Street.

COMO PARK, established in 1873, featured this Japanese garden in 1905. The park is one of more than a hundred in modern St. Paul. *Photograph by Sweet Studios, Minneapolis.*

SUMMIT AVENUE, St. Paul's tree-lined residential thoroughfare, was a wide street flanked by the imposing residences of industrial magnates when this photograph was taken in 1886.

ST. PAUL had become a railroad center by 1942 with skyscrapers looming above the banks of the Mississippi and the domes of the Catholic cathedral (left) and the Capitol (right) piercing the sky line.

MINNEAPOLIS had wooden sidewalks and unpaved streets when this view was photographed at Second Street and Nicollet Avenue in 1873. *Courtesy Minneapolis Public Library.*

MINNEAPOLIS grew rapidly after uniting with St. Anthony. This view, taken about 1900 from the corner of Washington and Second avenues, looks northeast across Nicollet Island toward old St. Anthony. The Exposition Building is on the river front at the right.

ROLLERS in a Minneapolis flour mill of the 1880s were used as a selling point in advertising its product. *Letterhead from the William Davidson Papers, May 18, 1883.*

THE FALLS OF ST. ANTHONY were threatened with destruction in October, 1869, and April, 1870, after an unsuccessful attempt was made to tunnel under Hennepin Island. Several breaks carried away huge sections of limestone and destroyed some of the mills.

THE STONE ARCH BRIDGE below the Falls of St. Anthony took the Great Northern Railroad into the heart of Minneapolis by the turn of the century. The Tenth Avenue Bridge is in the foreground, and the city's extensive milling district is visible in the background.

FLOUR MILLS AND ELEVATORS characterized the Minneapolis water front at the Falls of St. Anthony in the spring of 1950, when this picture was taken by Dave L. Jamison. *Courtesy Minneapolis Public Library.*

THE MINNEAPOLIS GRAIN EXCHANGE, established in 1888 by the Chamber of Commerce, contributed substantially to the city's leading position as a primary grain market. *Photograph taken about 1895.*

Two innovations stimulated the progress of the local flour mills — the introduction of the middlings purifier in 1870, and the substitution a few years later of rollers for grinding stones. These improvements resulted in lower production costs and a market that included Europe after 1878. The mills continued to expand until 1916, their peak year, when they produced twenty million barrels of flour. Thereafter, production declined. In 1920, Buffalo, New York, forged ahead of Minneapolis in flour production, and in the 1950s Kansas City took the lead.

Although Minneapolis won fame as the Mill City, its economy did not depend on flour alone. Metal and wood products became important by 1880, and after the turn of the century railroad and milling machinery and agricultural implements were manufactured on a large scale. Like its twin city ten miles downriver, Minneapolis also became a wholesaling center, specializing in clothing, furniture, drugs, groceries, fruits, and produce. After 1880, the city attained a lead over St. Paul in the financial world, and in 1914 it became the home of the ninth district Federal Reserve Bank. The leading processed items originating in Minneapolis today include food and related products, machinery and fabricated metal goods, electronics equipment, clothing and textiles, and printing.

Physically a city of great beauty, Minneapolis has within its limits a park system that embraces twenty-two lakes and some sixty miles of scenic drives. Its parks began humbly in 1857 with a tract of land presented by Edward Murphy. The foundations for true distinction, however, were laid between 1883 and 1890 when Charles M. Loring served as president of the park board. His farsighted planning and emphasis on civic improve-

NICOLLET AVENUE had become Minneapolis' principal retail thoroughfare by 1924. At its intersection with Eighth Street, a policeman regulated traffic with a hand-operated semaphore.

THE LAKE CALHOUN BATHING BEACH has long been
a popular feature of the Minneapolis park system.
In the second decade of the twentieth century,
when this picture was taken by Paul W. Cloud,
automobiles made it accessible to thousands.

THE MINNEAPOLIS SKY LINE of the early 1950s, dominated by the Foshay Tower, served as a dramatic
backdrop for Loring Park, which centers about one
of the smallest of the city's twoscore lakes.

ment are in large measure responsible for the city's impressive system, which includes nearly a hundred and fifty parks.

Duluth, far to the north and off the main path of settlement, was the latecomer among Minnesota's three major cities. After a modest start as a trading post on Minnesota Point in 1852, it displayed little capacity for growth until 1870, when it obtained a city charter. A short-lived period of prosperity, based on the new city's strategic position at the eastern terminal of the Northern Pacific Railroad, ended in 1873 with a financial panic that spelled failure for Jay Cooke, the road's promoter. In the decline that followed, Duluth lost its charter, but it obtained a new one in 1887. By this time it was evident that the westernmost location on the Great Lakes would become an important transportation and trading center for the hinterland to the north and west. A lighthouse on Minnesota Point warned incoming boats of an obstruction to traffic as early as 1858, and a ship canal cut in 1871 across the point near the Minnesota shore gave pioneering transports access to Duluth Harbor.

Grain and lumber, which constituted the bulk of the early shipments from the port, were supplemented after 1890 by a more distinctive commodity — iron ore from the newly discovered Mesabi Range deposits. It gave the city national significance as a funnel through which that strategic resource was dispatched to steel mills in the East. Before many years passed, Duluth was served by eight railroads, connecting it with ports on the Pacific and with cities in Canada and in southern Minnesota. Ore docks and grain elevators lined the city's harbor. Ships of specialized design — whalebacks, lumber hookers, packets, ore boats, automobile carriers, tankers — appeared on the water front between 1890 and 1950 as the nature of the cargo changed. Still another transformation may be expected when the St. Lawrence Seaway gives large Atlantic liners access to Duluth and Superior, adding to the nautical atmosphere of the mid-continental port which annually handles more tonnage than any in the United States except New York. Clinging to the steep banks of Lake Superior, modern Duluth extends northeastward along its shore for some twenty miles.

The rise of Minnesota's trio of populous cities after 1880 provides a local illustration of a national trend—the migration of people throughout America from rural areas to urban centers. The first census taken in Minnesota after statehood showed only 16,000 of its 172,000 people living in cities and villages. The proportion has increased steadily. At the turn of the century, 598,000 of the state's 1,751,000 people lived in urban communities; in 1940 the urban population almost equaled the rural; and by 1950 more than half of the state's 2,982,000 people were city dwellers. Most of them are concentrated in Minneapolis, St. Paul, Duluth, and their suburbs. Minneapolis, which counted 32,700 people in 1875, three years after its union with St. Anthony, passed St. Paul for the first time in 1880, with 46,000 people as compared with the capital city's 41,000. In a "census war" a decade later, both cities were guilty of padding their population figures; nevertheless, the breach widened, with Minneapolis some 30,000 ahead of St. Paul. In 1957, Minneapolis' population was estimated at 551,000, and St. Paul's at 339,000. Start-

211

DULUTH in 1872 consisted of wooden buildings on the steep banks bordering Lake Superior.

ing later, Duluth's growth has been slower. It showed a tenfold increase from 3,000 to 33,000 between 1870 and 1890, and it had 104,000 people in 1950. The rise of suburban communities near the major cities is characteristic of the years since 1940. St. Louis Park, Richfield, and Bloomington near Minneapolis, for example, now place among the state's six largest communities; the latter, which had only 3,600 people in 1940, counted 40,000 in 1957; White Bear Lake, once a summer resort north of St. Paul, showed a population growth in the same seventeen years from 2,800 to 12,000. Including such suburbs, Minnesota had more than thirty communities with over 10,000 residents by 1957.

Accompanying the rise of cities has been a growing industrialization which has radically changed the state's economic pattern. Traditionally, Minnesota was an agricultural state, dependent upon farming for its largest cash income. But the year 1948 marked a sharp break in the tradition when, for the first time, farm income fell behind personal income derived from manufacturing. Since that time the trend has continued, and by 1956 there was a gap of $465,000,000. In order of value, Minnesota's chief industries in 1954 were concerned with food, machinery, paper and pulp, printing and publishing, and chemical products. In 1850 only one per cent of the state's total population was engaged in manufacturing; by 1890 the figure had jumped to more than five per cent; and by 1954 almost ten per cent were employed in manufacturing industries. In the three

212

THE DULUTH WATER FRONT of the early 1870s reflected a prosperity that grew out of the shipment of grain and lumber over steel rails and on lake boats. *Photograph by Illingworth.*

WHALEBACKS were a unique feature of the Great Lakes trade in the 1890s. The smaller of the two shown below was a barge. In the background may be seen the incline railroad which connected the Duluth water front with the residential section above. *Courtesy St. Louis County Historical Society.*

major metropolitan areas, 48,199 wage earners depended upon manufacturing firms for their livelihood in 1900; in 1954 the total had soared to 151,974—in increase of almost three hundred per cent.

With the shift from agriculture to manufacturing, Minnesota had provided an expanding theater of activity for labor. Its organizations became a factor in the state's economy as early as the 1850s, when typographical unions were founded in both St. Paul and Minneapolis. They were followed in succeeding decades by unions of plasterers, painters, plumbers, cigar makers, and trainmen. By 1883 the Knights of Labor, a national secret society which attempted to unite all workers, had organized in Minnesota on a state-wide basis, and it not only receives credit for Minnesota's first Labor Day celebration in 1885, but it also helped establish the Minnesota State Federation of Labor in 1890. Ten years later the state had 206 labor groups with 17,625 members. By 1954 the American Federation of Labor had an estimated Minnesota membership of 136,000, and more than seventy-five per cent of the state's workers were unionized. Their role in Minnesota politics attained importance in 1930, when the Farmer-Labor party won an election for the first time.

Although the bulk of Minnesota's industrial plants and the majority of its laborers are concentrated in its three large cities, some important manufacturing firms operate in the state's less populous communities. A few are mentioned in the chapter that follows.

213

AN AERIAL BRIDGE, built in 1905, spans the ship canal leading to Duluth-Superior Harbor. The original, shown at the left, with its suspended car that carried passengers and vehicles across the channel, was the only one of its type in the United States. It was changed to a lift bridge in 1929. *Photograph by Gallagher's Studio, Duluth, 1926; courtesy St. Louis County Historical Society.*

SUPERIOR STREET, the principal business thoroughfare in Duluth, looked like this at its intersection with Fifth Avenue about 1900.

THE MODERN PORT OF DULUTH is a meeting
point for rail and water transportation. *Photograph by V. P. Hollis, about 1938.*

215

22.

Main Street
in Transition

THE PROGRESS of Minnesota's less populous communities has been distinguished by a movement in the direction of urban living and industrialization similiar to, though perhaps less marked than, that which characterized the growth of the state's three major cities. Some of the townsites established in the nineteenth century fulfilled the expectations of their enthusiastic promoters, and many a settlement that once catered only to the needs of neighboring farmers experienced a radical transformation. One became a world-famous medical center; others grew after rails and roads crossed the state, and the resources of near-by areas were exploited; many attracted manufacturing plants that serve a national market.

In the decades that followed the Civil War, signs of change became evident in the towns founded during the territorial era in southern Minnesota, and in time some attained distinction and even fame. Fairmont attracted a colony of fox-hunting Britons; Northfield became the home of two colleges; Faribault began to produce blankets that sold over a wide area; Austin and Albert Lea acquired meat-packing plants and became leading industrial centers in rich and diversified agricultural areas; Owatonna gave rise to a business which supplies pins, rings, trophies, and emblems for schools and colleges in all parts of the United States.

The most widely known community in the entire state, however, is Rochester. Its transition from a small agricultural town to a great medical center comprises a unique chapter in the history of Minnesota's main streets. Beginning as a transportation hub in a rich wheat-raising area, it attracted a pioneering physician, Dr. William Worrall Mayo. An offer by the Sisters of St. Francis to build and maintain a hospital if he would staff it resulted in the opening of St. Mary's Hospital in 1889. This simple three-story structure, equipped with a single private room and forty beds in three wards, was the nucleus about which grew the great Mayo Clinic of 1958. A small building erected in 1914 was replaced in 1929 by a slender skyscraper, and this in turn gave way in 1954

216

to a twelve-story establishment that occupies an entire block. The old doctor's sons, Drs. William J. and Charles H. Mayo, organized the Mayo Foundation in 1915 and established its connection with the medical school of the University of Minnesota. More than six hundred physicians receive graduate training at Rochester each year, and patients by the thousands from all parts of the world annually seek treatment there. Rochester's population, estimated at thirty-five thousand in 1957, is larger than that of any other Minnesota community outside the three major cities and their suburbs.

As this medical mecca and its neighboring communities matured, the river towns of southern Minnesota also developed. Among those on the Mississippi between the Iowa border and the head of navigation, Winona took the lead. After beginning as a lumber and wheat-shipping port, it attracted twenty-four factories by the turn of the century and eighty-two plants by 1957. Notable among them is a firm that distributes from door to door on an international scale some three hundred products, including medicines, foods, and cosmetics. Upstream, Red Wing became a prosperous center of somewhat smaller scope; one of its industrial plants has been producing pottery since 1877. Like Winona, Red Wing continued to grow after railroad transportation replaced steamboat traffic. With that change, however, some once prosperous river towns, like Read's Landing, faded into insignificance.

SAUK CENTRE'S MAIN STREET was lined with small shops in 1925, shortly after a native son, Sinclair Lewis, used it as a setting for a novel that became a best seller. *Courtesy* St. Paul Dispatch-Pioneer Press.

TWO HARBORS, incorporated as a village in 1888, became an important Lake Superior port for ore shipments after iron was discovered on the Vermilion Range. One of the earliest ore docks built there appears at the right in the picture above.

A SALOON which catered to newly arrived Scandinavian settlers and the shop of a dealer in farm machinery stood side by side on Alexandria's main street in 1876. *Photograph by Trenham.*

WABASHA, on the Mississippi at the foot of Lake Pepin, boasted a main street flanked by shops in 1870, about three decades after it was founded. *Photograph by Upton.*

HENDERSON, founded in 1852 on the Minnesota River in Sibley County, celebrated the Fourth of July in 1893 with a parade on its main street. Participating in the procession were Civil War veterans and members of the local fire department.

HIBBING, founded in 1892, was moved between 1918 and 1921 from its original site over a rich ore deposit. *Photograph taken in 1921; courtesy St. Louis County Historical Society.*

ASKOV, originally called Partridge, was founded before 1890 on cutover land on the Great Northern near Hinckley. *Photograph taken in 1908; courtesy Pine County Historical Society, Pine City.*

BEMIDJI'S Third Street retained its frontier atmosphere in 1897, a year after the town was platted on a site once occupied by a Chippewa village. *Courtesy Beltrami County Historical Society, Bemidji.*

Along the Minnesota, Le Sueur has a canning factory that makes available throughout the nation produce raised by local farmers; St. Peter is the home of a state hospital and a liberal arts college; Mankato has developed as a manufacturing, transportation, and wholesaling center; New Ulm Germans established breweries and extensive food-processing plants; Redwood Falls, a trading town, and Granite Falls, in a quarrying area, evolved about water-power sites. Unlike many Mississippi and Minnesota River communities, those on the St. Croix did not fulfill the promise of their early years, declining as the pine forests of the valley were exhausted. Stillwater, once classed with St. Paul and St. Anthony as one of Minnesota's three chief centers of population, had fewer people in 1950 than in 1880; Marine-on-St. Croix, which cradled the state's infant saw-milling industry, is now a sleepy town of about three hundred residents.

In the wake of railroads reaching toward the Pacific, new towns began to dot Minnesota's northern and western counties. Brainerd, gateway to a large resort area, was founded in 1870 at the point where the Northern Pacific crosses the Mississippi; by 1882, Fergus Falls, now the largest city in western Minnesota, had both that line and the St. Paul and Pacific, later the Great Northern; the same roads stimulated the growth of Breckenridge and Moorhead on the Red River. A plant in the latter community which manufactures beet sugar is one of three such factories in the Red River Valley. The first was established at East Grand Forks in 1926, and the third was erected at Crookston as late as 1954. They provide a market for one of the state's major agricultural products. Lumbermen exploiting the northern forests had much to do with the founding of settlements like Walker and Bemidji, which are now resort centers. Grand Rapids on the upper Mississippi, International Falls on the Rainy River and the Canadian boundary, and Cloquet on the St. Louis River became the sites of huge mills which are in large measure responsible for Minnesota's pulp and paper production.

The later decades of the nineteenth century saw the growth of new communities on the iron-mining frontier of the Arrowhead country. Some, like Ely and Winton near the Vermilion Range discoveries of the 1880s and Hibbing and Virginia on the Mesabi, were for a time both mining and lumbering centers; others, like Eveleth and Biwabik, began in the 1890s after the Mesabi deposits were found. Two Harbors, the Lake Superior terminal of the Duluth, Missabe and Iron Range Railroad, became a shipping point for eastward bound ore and lumber.

The industrial transition of Minnesota's main streets has been accompanied by other changes. Retail trade took on a new aspect as general stores, once the centers of social and economic life, were supplanted by specialty shops and supermarkets; saloons gave way to liquor stores and cocktail bars; sophisticated entertainment that once could be enjoyed only in large cities reached the motion picture theaters of the most remote villages; garages replaced blacksmith shops as the automobile precipitated a revolution in transportation. How such transformations altered the physical appearance of the varied communities scattered throughout Minnesota is suggested by the accompanying views taken on local main streets.

LIVERY STABLES, like this one at St. Charles in 1907, made local transportation available to the people who lived on main street in the preautomobile era.

THE BLACKSMITH was an important figure on main street in horse-and-buggy days. This one was in business at Le Center about 1895. *Courtesy Mrs. James Lumex, Le Center.*

THIS SALOON, with its characteristic bar, beer kegs and measuring cans, cigar display case, stove, and spittoons prospered in Rochester in the late 1880s. *Courtesy Olmsted County Historical Society, Rochester.*

222

THE LOBBY of the Minnesota House at St. Cloud displayed a sign in 1876 announcing that "Persons without baggage must pay in advance." *Courtesy Miss Gertrude Gove, St. Cloud.*

HOTELS which catered to tourists became a feature of main streets in the resort centers of Hubbard and Becker counties in the 1880s. An example is the Hotel Minnesota at Detroit Lakes. *Photograph by Dr. L. C. Weeks, Detroit Lakes.*

GENERAL STORES like this one, opened at West Newton in 1871, served as shopping and social gathering places. *Photograph taken in 1951; courtesy* St. Paul Dispatch-Pioneer Press.

A MEAT MARKET at Blue Earth was operated about 1900 by a butcher who displayed carcasses beside hams and sausages. *Courtesy Faribault County Historical Society, Blue Earth.*

THE BARBER attracted a growing clientele as life on main street became more sophisticated. This one, who ran a shop in Rochester about 1895, needed two assistants. *Courtesy Olmsted County Historical Society.*

DRUGSTORES had soda fountains and stationery counters by the early years of the present century, when this shop served the people of St. Cloud. *Courtesy Miss Gove.*

A GROCERY STORE at White Bear Lake was equipped with bins and jars in 1894. Dried fruits were displayed in packing boxes and canned goods lined the shelves behind the counter.

LADIES' HATS were large and ornate about 1910, when this St. Peter shop prospered. *Courtesy Nicollet County Historical Society, St. Peter.*

DEPARTMENT STORES and specialty shops replaced general stores in larger centers. This lace and ribbon counter was in a retail establishment at Mankato about 1900.

A TYPICAL HARDWARE STORE at Owatonna about 1900 handled a stock of household articles that ranged all the way from mouse traps and scales to washing machines.

BREWERIES prospered in many of Minnesota's small towns. This large plant, photographed about 1890, flourished at Mantorville. *Courtesy Dodge County Historical Society.*

227

THE RED WING STONEWARE COMPANY was the earliest of three firms that consolidated soon after 1900 to become Red Wing Potteries. The company's products are sold throughout the nation. *Lithograph, about 1883; courtesy Red Wing Potteries.*

BRICKMAKING became an important industry in the Princeton area, where good clay was plentiful. This brickyard was established at near-by Brickton in 1889.

THE STOCKYARDS at South St. Paul, established in 1887, made the community one of the nation's leading livestock markets. By 1920, when this photograph was taken, it was giving employment to thousands of laborers.

A PAPER MILL at International Falls processes pulpwood cut on both sides of the Canadian boundary, here marked by the Rainy River. Fort Frances is located across the border on the stream's north bank. *Photograph taken in 1953; courtesy Minnesota Division of Publicity, St. Paul.*

MOORHEAD in the Red River Valley is the
home of this beet sugar manufacturing plant
built in 1948. *Photograph taken in 1956;
courtesy Clay County Historical Society.*

WINONA on the Mississippi, after beginning modestly in the 1850s, became an important industrial center, ranking ninth in size among Minnesota cities in 1950. *Courtesy Winona County Historical Society, Winona.*

MARINE-ON-ST. CROIX, the site of Minnesota's earliest sawmill, is now a tiny village. Almost deserted in winter, its scenic attractions draw summer tourists. *Photograph by Dunn, 1918.*

231

23.

Achieving
Cultural Maturity

THE CULTURAL ASSETS that distinguish Minnesota have their roots in the period between 1865 and the turn of the century, when the state emerged from its frontier status and developed into a modern commonwealth. The second-generation Minnesotans who grew up there after the Civil War found many of the problems that had occupied the pioneers solved, and consequently they had more leisure than their fathers for recreation, and more time for education and for self-expression in art, music, and literature.

To meet the needs of this new generation, secondary schools were established by the legislatures of 1878 and 1881. By 1900, one out of every twenty Minnesota youngsters attended high school. The proportion increased until in 1930 three out of five were enrolled, and in 1950 eighty-seven per cent of all Minnesotans ranging in age from fourteen to seventeen were in school.

On the elementary level, twentieth-century education in Minnesota has been marked by a sharp drop in the number of pupils attending ungraded schools like those in which their pioneer forebears learned the three Rs, and by a corresponding rise in enrollment for consolidated and urban schools. The consolidation of school districts under a law of 1947 resulted in a reduction from 7,606 to 3,298 within a single decade.

To provide opportunities for high school graduates who wished to continue their educations, colleges were needed. In addition to an embryo state university, by 1860 Minnesota had a normal school at Winona—the first institution of its kind west of the Mississippi. Others were established between 1868 and 1919 at Mankato, Moorhead, St. Cloud, Duluth, and Bemidji. That at Duluth became a branch of the university in 1947; the remaining five still exist as state colleges. In 1958 Minnesota also had nine junior and fourteen accredited private colleges. Among the latter are Carleton, established under Congregational auspices at Northfield in 1867; St. Olaf, founded in the same community by Norwegian Lutherans in 1874; Gustavus Adolphus, opened by Swedish Lutherans at Red Wing in 1862 and removed to St. Peter in 1874; Macalester, which has

232

ONE-ROOM COUNTRY SCHOOLS, like this one near Fosston in 1895, provided education for Minnesota's rural youth before 1900.

THE MADISON SCHOOL was one of St. Paul's larger elementary plants in 1911, when the photograph below was taken by C. P. Gibson.

flourished as a Presbyterian college in St. Paul since 1885; and a number of Catholic institutions of higher learning, including St. Thomas in St. Paul and St. Scholastica in Duluth, both of which began in the late nineteenth century.

The total enrollment in these and other private colleges is a far cry from the figure for the University of Minnesota, which had nearly 26,000 students on three campuses at Minneapolis, St. Paul, and Duluth in the autumn of 1957. This gigantic institution evolved from the little preparatory school of 217 pupils that William W. Folwell found near the Falls of St. Anthony when he arrived to become its president in 1869. After Cyrus Northrop became its head in 1884, he added to the original liberal arts program, establishing colleges of engineering, law, and medicine, and a department of agriculture with an experimental farm. The university's physical plant expanded rapidly after 1900, until at the beginning of 1958 it embraced fourteen units in widely separated sections of the state.

Among the eighty-five buildings on the main campus is a library erected in 1924, which houses more than 1,800,000 volumes — the largest single accumulation of books in Minnesota. The private library assembled by James J. Hill was opened to the public in St. Paul in 1921. Both St. Paul and Minneapolis have comprehensive public libraries that can trace their beginnings to private associations of the 1850s. Today they are among the more than two hundred public libraries which serve Minnesotans. One of the most extensive Americana collections in the Midwest, comprising more than 225,000 volumes, has been assembled by the Minnesota Historical Society since that institution was founded in 1849. Other Minnesota libraries devoted to special subjects include the scientific collections of the Ramsey and Hennepin County Medical societies and the

PIGTAILS, pinafores, stationary desks, and blackboards characterized the typical elementary classroom in Minnesota's schools at the turn of the century. *Photograph taken in Maxfield School, St. Paul, 1904.*

ELEMENTARY SCHOOLS of the 1950s have light, cheerful classrooms with attractive, movable furnishings. *Photograph taken in Waite Park School, Minneapolis, 1951; courtesy Magney, Tusler, and Setter, Minneapolis.*

HIGH SCHOOLS of elaborate design, like this one completed at Hibbing in 1923, were erected in the Mesabi Range mining towns. *Courtesy Minnesota Division of Publicity.*

THE ST. CLOUD NORMAL SCHOOL, established in 1869, trained science teachers of the 1890s in a biology laboratory that was then considered well equipped. *Photograph by E. S. Hill.*

THE UNIVERSITY OF MINNESOTA consisted of a dozen modestly designed buildings grouped about the knoll on the Minneapolis campus in 1901, when this picture was taken by Sweet Studios.

GUSTAVUS ADOLPHUS COLLEGE at St. Peter (left), founded by the Swedish Lutheran church, is typical of Minnesota's sectarian colleges. *Photograph taken in 1927.*

A MODERN LIBRARY was completed in 1956 on the campus of Carleton College, which was founded shortly after the Civil War. *Courtesy Magney, Tusler, and Setter.*

THE MINNESOTA HISTORICAL SOCIETY, the oldest cultural institution in the state, houses in its St. Paul building a definitive Americana library, a museum, and extensive collections of manuscripts, pictures, and newspapers. *Photograph by Eugene D. Becker, 1955.*

Mayo Clinic, the Ames Library of South Asia in St. Paul, and scores of smaller libraries assembled to meet the needs of individual business concerns.

As the cultural interests of Minnesotans widened, they acquired a taste for more sophisticated entertainment than could be provided by occasional minstrel or variety shows, itinerant troupes traveling in medicine wagons to advertise patent cure-alls, moving panoramas, sword swallowers and snake charmers who displayed their freakish skills in dime museums, and family musical troupes. With the development of a dependable audience and the improvement of transportation facilities, top-ranking actors and musicians booked engagements in the upper Midwest. Joseph Jefferson played before Twin City audiences as early as 1884, appearing in *Rip Van Winkle* and other classics; towering giants of the American theater like Edwin Booth, E. H. Sothern, Julia Marlowe, and Richard Mansfield presented Shakespearean repertoire; Maude Adams charmed Minnesota audiences in *The Little Minister* and *Peter Pan;* and Mrs. Patrick Campbell shocked them in *The Second Mrs. Tanqueray.*

Stages aplenty for such productions were available throughout Minnesota. Minneapolis' pioneer Pence Opera House of 1867 soon encountered competition from the Academy of Music and the Grand Opera House. St. Paul was booking plays at both the Metropolitan and the Grand Opera houses by 1890, and Duluth had a well-equipped Grand Opera House. The Philharmonic Hall at Winona seated seven hundred people, and opera houses at Crookston, Moorhead, St. Cloud, and Wadena accommodated five hundred drama enthusiasts each. Among other Minnesota communities that could boast of playhouses in the 1880s were Stillwater, Hastings, Red Wing, and Brainerd. They continued to flourish well into the second decade of the present century, when motion pictures began to replace legitimate productions in all but the largest population centers.

Unlike drama, music has continued to play a major role in the lives of thousands of Minnesotans. Ole Bull's successful Minnesota appearances between 1856 and 1873 encouraged other artists to venture into the West, and in time he was followed by most of the major musicians who graced the concert stage of the late nineteenth and early twentieth centuries. The names and accomplishments of Theodore Thomas, Lillian Nordica, and Enrico Caruso were familiar to Minnesotans long before phonographs and radios carried music into their homes. The Schubert Club founded in St. Paul in 1882 and the Thursday Musical organized in Minneapolis a decade later promoted the musical interests of their respective communities. St. Paul's German pioneers established a musical society which had two hundred members in 1863. After George Seibert became its director in 1870, he organized an orchestra which played an important role in the state's cultural life, giving concerts and furnishing music for operas, plays, religious services, balls, and banquets in many localities.

From St. Paul's German community emerged the individuals who in large measure were responsible for the birth of the Minneapolis Symphony Orchestra — Frank Danz, senior and junior, and Emil Oberhoffer. Among its forebears was the Philharmonic Club, known originally as the Filharmonix, a choral organization which had three hun-

238

AN AMATEUR THEATRICAL GROUP performed "The War of the Roses" before audiences that assembled in Minneapolis and Waseca in 1894.

WONDERLAND, a Minneapolis dime museum, was advertised as a "shelter for nature's oddities" and an "anchorage for the world's marvels." *Photograph by Arthur B. Rugg, 1896.*

MEDICINE SHOWS, like this one staged by a Kickapoo Indian group, traveled through Minnesota giving entertainments while selling patent remedies. *Photograph taken at Marine about 1890; courtesy J. T. Dunn.*

dred members and had obtained Oberhoffer's services as director by 1900. Its desperate need for a dependable, professional orchestra gave Minnesota its greatest musical asset three years later. The new symphony orchestra—the eighth major organization of its type to be established in the United States—made its debut on the evening of November 5 with the inspired Oberhoffer on the podium, Frank Danz, Jr., in the concertmaster's chair, many of the men from the latter's orchestra at key desks, and Marcella Sembrich as soloist. After performing in various rented halls, the orchestra found a permanent home at Northrop Auditorium on the campus of the University of Minnesota in 1929. Oberhoffer headed the organization until 1922; his successors include Eugene Ormandy, Dimitri Mitropoulos, and Antal Dorati. On tours, this organization of almost a hundred skilled musicians has carried its message of Midwest cultural attainment to many sections of North America, as well as to Europe and, in the autumn of 1957, as far as the Middle East.

Various other groups and activities give evidence of the musical interest and ability of numerous Minnesotans. As early as 1884, a family concert troupe from the St. Peter area organized the Andrews Opera Company, which for almost two decades produced such classics as *Carmen* and *Faust* in towns large and small throughout the Middle and Far West. The choir organized by F. Melius Christiansen at St. Olaf College after he joined its faculty in 1903 has achieved international renown. St. Paul had its own symphony orchestra from 1906 to 1914, and for many years thereafter Minneapolis shared its orchestra with the capital city. The St. Paul Civic Opera marked its twenty-fifth anniversary in 1958, and the Duluth Symphony Orchestra was founded in 1934.

A taste for the fine arts among Minnesotans bore fruit somewhat later than did their interest in music. The Minneapolis Society of Fine Arts, incorporated in 1883, arranged loan exhibits and established a school of art. Business leaders who made fortunes in Minnesota, like James J. Hill and Thomas B. Walker, began to assemble collections of the works of the masters. Walker shared his treasures with others by opening his gallery to the public in 1894; a building erected to house it in 1927 became known as the Walker Art Center, which since 1939 has specialized in contemporary art. The most im-

THE SWISS BELL RINGING COMPANY of the four Trousdale brothers was on tour in 1896.

240

THEATERGOERS thronged to St. Paul's Metropolitan Opera House about the turn of the century to see Maude Adams star in such popular successes as *The Little Minister* and *Peter Pan*.

JOHN STEVENS, working in this studio at Rochester, produced a moving panorama depicting events of the Sioux War which became a popular entertainment feature after 1868. *Photograph taken about 1865; courtesy Olmsted County Historical Society.*

THE PENCE OPERA HOUSE, at Hennepin Avenue and Second Street, was the cultural and entertainment center of Minneapolis after it opened in 1867. *Photograph by Illingworth.*

A BAND organized and directed by Frank Danz, Jr., in the 1880s was among the ancestors of the Minneapolis Symphony. In this photograph, taken about 1886, Danz, wearing a derby, is in the center of the second row.

THE ST. PAUL AUDITORIUM, completed in 1907, functioned as a theater, a concert hall, and a convention arena. This view of the Fifth Street entrance probably dates from 1908, when the St. Paul Symphony Orchestra, advertised on the poster, was giving a concert series there. *Photograph by Truman W. Ingersoll; courtesy Library of Congress.*

THE MINNEAPOLIS SYMPHONY ORCHESTRA performed under Oberhoffer's baton at the Minneapolis Auditorium, later the Lyceum Theater, from 1905 to 1922. *Photograph taken about 1918.*

OBERHOFFER was a "portrait of elegance" when he mounted the podium in the Exposition Building to direct the symphony orchestra's first concert. *Photograph by Joseph Opsahl in the first program.*

THE PROGRAM for the orchestra's initial appearance, on November 5, 1903, displayed this cover and included such numbers as Schubert's "Unfinished" symphony and Liszt's "Les Préludes."

THE
MINNEAPOLIS
SYMPHONY
ORCHESTRA

THE
PHILHARMONIC
CLUB

FIRST ORCHESTRAL CONCERT
NOVEMBER 5, 1903.

243

portant and extensive art collection in Minnesota and the Northwest is that of the Minneapolis Institute of Arts, which was founded in 1911.

Other manifestations of a concern for art among Minnesotans are to be found in exhibits on view from time to time in the American-Swedish Institute of Minneapolis, the St. Paul Gallery and School of Art, and the University Gallery in Northrop Auditorium. Museums which promote special interests include those of the Minnesota Historical Society in St. Paul and of more than sixty local organizations devoted to state history; the St. Paul Science Museum, which stresses Minnesota archaeology; the Duluth Children's Museum; and the natural history museum of the University of Minnesota.

Minnesota's activities in the fields of music, art, and drama, and in building collections of books and art objects, have long been bearing fruit. The state, for example, has given to the world some widely famed literary figures. A pioneer among them was Ignatius Donnelly, whose *Atlantis* and *The Great Cryptogram* were best sellers of the 1880s. With the new century, Minnesota produced creative writers of far-reaching influence — including Sinclair Lewis, the first American to win the Nobel Prize for literature, whose *Main Street* inaugurated a new trend in fiction; F. Scott Fitzgerald, recorder of the "jazz age" and its foibles; and O. E. Rölvaag, whose *Giants in the Earth* and its sequels have been described as the "great pioneer saga" of America. Scores of other writers whose varied careers began in Minnesota include Charles Flandrau, Thorstein Veblen, Martha Ostenso, Maud Hart Lovelace, Norman Katkov, Eric Sevareid, Thomas Heggen, and Max Shulman. Only a few of the artists whose accomplishments in other fields have enriched American life can be mentioned here. Notable among them are Alexis Jean Fournier, George Plowman, Wanda Gág, Levon West, and Adolph Dehn, painters and etchers; Paul Manship, Jacob and Paul Fjelde, and John Rood, sculptors; Cass Gilbert, Leroy S. Buffington, and William G. Purcell, architects; Cecil Yapp, Gale Sondergaard, and Blanche Jurka, actors; and Olive Fremstad, Florence Macbeth, and George Meader, musicians. Out of the eager and enthusiastic cultural activities that characterized Minnesota's first century of statehood have evolved these talents, which mark the maturity of the commonwealth.

SINCLAIR LEWIS, who attained lasting fame with the publication of *Main Street* in 1920, is Minnesota's foremost literary figure. This photograph was taken in the year that saw the appearance of his first best seller. *Courtesy* St. Paul Dispatch-Pioneer Press.

THE WALKER COLLECTION, assembled by a Minnesota lumberman, was on display in a wing of his Minneapolis mansion when this picture was taken about 1918.

PAUL MANSHIP'S "Indian Hunter and His Dog," in Cochran Memorial Park, Summit and Western, St. Paul, is the work of a native Minnesotan. He completed the group in 1926. *From a signed model in the Women's City Club of St. Paul; photograph by Becker, 1958.*

THE MINNEAPOLIS INSTITUTE OF ARTS, founded in 1911, has influenced the art tastes of Minnesotans by making available a permanent collection and traveling shows of high quality. *Photograph taken in 1939.*

24.

Minnesotans
at Play

IN THE LATER DECADES of the nineteenth century, Americans were learning to indulge in the organized sports that one historian has termed the "safety valve" of an industrial society. Minnesotans followed the general trend by turning to outdoor recreation. Fads such as croquet and bicycling swept the country and filtered westward. The League of American Wheelmen, organized in 1880 at Newport, Rhode Island, had a Minnesota branch within two years. Golf and tennis made their national debuts in the 1870s and 1880s, and in the same decades baseball games, horse and boat races, boxing matches, and prize fights were attracting crowds of enthusiastic spectators. All became popular in Minnesota.

Interest in the "royal game of golf," for example, was closely associated with the rise of country clubs, which began to appear in Minnesota as early as 1888. In that year the Town and Country Club of St. Paul was established, and ten years later a group of Minneapolis men organized under the name Minikahda. Within another year Duluth had an association with facilities for archery, tennis, trapshooting, sleighing, skiing, and tobogganing, as well as golf. The latter, however, remained the chief interest of members of country clubs, and in time numerous public and municipal courses were established in the state. By 1957 Minnesota's golf enthusiasts had at their disposal no fewer than 150 public and private courses.

For the promotion of individual sports, other organizations came into being in great variety. St. Paul had a boat club as early as 1870 and Duluth followed suit in 1886; three curling groups were active in the state in the 1890s; a hunting lodge at Hallock was a rendezvous for sportsmen from the East in the 1880s. With the growth of motor transportation, automobile associations were organized after 1900, more than a hundred existing in the state at the height of their popularity; athletic clubs for city dwellers opened in Minneapolis in 1915 and in St. Paul in 1918. The nation's pioneer ski group was organized by Norwegian settlers at Red Wing in 1883, half a century before this

246

CROQUET was one of the earliest outdoor games to become popular in Minnesota. This stereograph of a court in the yard of a Lake Minnetonka cottage was made about 1880 by Jacoby.

THE FLOUR CITY CYCLISTS' CLUBHOUSE at 1611 Park Avenue, Minneapolis, was a popular rendezvous for bicycle enthusiasts of the 1880s and 1890s.

exciting winter pastime acquired appeal for large numbers of Minnesotans. Among other immigrant groups who brought their sports with them from Europe were the Czechs and the Germans, whose Sokol and Turnverein organizations specialized in gymnastic achievement. The New Ulm Turnverein had other objectives, too, for it staged elaborate theatrical performances, formed a singing section, gave costume balls, and supported a fire department.

Winter sports received a boost in 1886 when the first St. Paul ice carnival was staged, ostensibly to correct a general belief that Minnesota was a "hyperborean region where existence is a burden during the winter months." Repeated in several succeeding seasons, the carnivals, which centered about glittering ice palaces with skating rinks and toboggan slides near by, attracted thousands to the Minnesota capital. In 1916 the winter festival was revived, and it soon became an annual event featuring parades and sports like skiing and skating. A contrasting summer festival, the Minneapolis Aquatennial, has been taking advantage of the city's lakes to feature water sports each July since 1940.

THE GERMANIA TURNVEREIN of St. Paul sent this uniformed troupe to Duluth for a gymnastic festival in 1892. *Photograph by Ingersoll.*

TALLYHO RIDES to outlying points were arranged by groups eager for outdoor recreation. An example is this Fort Snelling excursion of 1892. *Courtesy State Historical Society of Wisconsin.*

THE MINIKAHDA CLUB of Minneapolis had tennis courts near the first tee of its golf course, and both were close to its pretentious clubhouse. *Photograph by Sweet Studios, 1901.*

THE TOWN AND COUNTRY CLUB of St. Paul provided facilities for social events as well as for participating sports like golf and tennis. *Photograph by Sweet Studios, 1908.*

BIG GAME HUNTERS from New York were photographed by William Hartvig in 1889 in front of the sportsmen's lodge built in 1880 by Charles Hallock in the Kittson County resort town which is named for him.

DUCKS and other types of waterfowl were abundant and large bags were the rule in the 1890s, when hunting for market as well as for sport was still legal in Minnesota. *Stereograph, courtesy Library of Congress.*

THE MINNESOTA BOAT CLUB, organized in 1870, centered its activities about a clubhouse on Raspberry Island in the Mississippi at St. Paul. *Montage picturing the club's membership in 1884–85.*

A NATIONAL SKI TOURNAMENT was held in February, 1928, at Red Wing, where pioneers who imported the sport from Norway organized the first ski club in the United States in the early 1880s. *Photograph by Steaffens Studio, Red Wing.*

251

THE ST. PAUL ICE PALACE of 1888 was erected in Central Park for the city's third annual winter carnival. Winter sports of various types, horse races on the frozen Mississippi, theatrical performances, fancy-dress balls, concerts, and parades were among the events connected with this festival exploiting Minnesota's season of snow and ice.

AN ICE-FISHING CONTEST on White Bear Lake was a spectacular feature of the 1955 winter carnival. *Courtesy Minnesota Division of Publicity.*

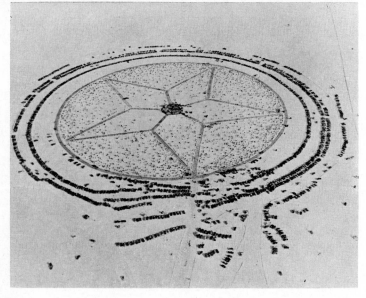

Outdoor summer activities like boating and swimming, which depend upon Minnesota's more than eleven thousand lakes, helped to promote the founding of resorts. They first attained importance in the state shortly after the Civil War, and their rise in the years that followed was greatly stimulated by a widespread belief that Minnesota's climate was beneficial to invalids. As the state became known for the "health-restoring properties" of its "cold, dry, invigorating air," health-seekers, particularly consumptives, made their way northward by the thousands. To accommodate these newcomers, hotels, boardinghouses, "retreats for invalids," and resorts were established in growing numbers. The Winslow House, once a popular St. Anthony hostelry, was transformed into the Western Hygiean Home for Invalids; the Oak Grove House at Cedar Lake invited health-seekers to partake of its hospitality; hotels erected at White Bear Lake and Lake Minnetonka, within easy reach of the state's largest cities, let it be known that they could make invalids comfortable.

These resort hotels soon became popular among Minnesotans seeking relief from city heat, as well as with tourists from the South and East. In 1881 people from New York, Missouri, Kansas, and Iowa were registered at Minnetonka hotels. By that time resorts had been opened also at Lake Elmo, Prior Lake, the Dalles of the St. Croix, Lake St. Croix, and Frontenac, which was described as the "Newport of the Northwest." These establishments, most of which catered to visitors searching for health as well as pleasure, were the forerunners of some forty-five hundred resorts which welcomed vacationing tourists to Minnesota in the mid-twentieth century.

Fishing was perhaps the most popular pastime among early visitors. Many a sportsman chose to vacation in Minnesota after hearing reports of fabulous catches like that of a party which landed eighty black bass and thirty pickerel in two hours on Lake Minnetonka. As such exploitation depleted the stocks in the lakes of the south, sportsmen followed the railroads into the less settled northern part of the state, where both fish and game continued in plentiful supply until long after the advent of the automobile made that area easily accessible. More than three hundred thousand fishermen from other states now visit Minnesota each year, and well over a million residents purchased fishing licenses in 1956.

In order to broadcast information to tourists throughout the nation, the Ten Thousand Lakes of Minnesota Association was organized in 1916, and in 1923 the Minnesota Arrowhead Association was founded to advertise the beauties and advantages of the state's northeastern section with its Lake Superior shore and unique border wilderness. There, in the nation's largest national forest, twentieth-century voyageurs find complete seclusion and escape from the industrial world and its problems. With canoes as the only means of transportation, they can paddle for days on end over lakes and streams bordered by stately pines, portaging between waterways and camping under the stars at night. The state tourist bureau and the Ten Thousand Lakes and Arrowhead associations have distributed tons of literature about Minnesota's resorts, its canoe country, and its state parks. The beginning of the extensive system of parks that flourishes in

PARADES like this procession of 1956 on Nicollet Avenue mark the Minneapolis Aquatennial, which stresses summer recreation, chiefly water sports. *Courtesy Minneapolis Aquatennial.*

THE AQUA FOLLIES, staged for the annual Minneapolis Aquatennial, features a water ballet and performances by well-known diving and swimming stars. *Courtesy Minneapolis Aquatennial.*

modern Minnesota can be traced to 1891, when Itasca State Park, which embraces the source of the Mississippi, was founded as a result of the persistent and devoted efforts of Jacob V. Brower, its first superintendent. Itasca is not only the oldest but the largest of the thirty-eight state parks that preserve areas of special historical or scenic interest throughout the commonwealth in 1958.

Spectator sports, amateur and professional, have long received enthusiastic support in Minnesota. An example is horse racing, which reached a climax in the exploits of the great pacer, Dan Patch, after he was purchased by M. W. Savage of Minneapolis in 1902. The popularity of this unique animal may be judged from the fact that 93,000 spectators watched his performance at the Minnesota State Fair of 1906, when he paced a mile in 1:55 — a record that has never been broken. Amateur baseball teams, some of which were active in Minnesota as early as 1857, began to play competitive games about 1865. Only a year after the pioneering National League of Baseball Clubs was organized in New York in 1876, the Minneapolis organization made its bow to the Northwest. A decade later, both St. Paul and Minneapolis could boast of professional teams, which under the nicknames of "Millers" and "Saints" have become local institutions. Beginning in the 1890s, basketball figured in the althetic programs of Minnesota secondary schools and colleges. With the growing popularity of the game, the Mill City acquired a professional team known as the "Lakers" in 1947.

It was football, however, that was first developed to a high degree after athletic activity became important in Minnesota colleges. Although students in the University of Minnesota played the game as early as 1878, they did not compete with teams from other states until 1890. During several decades games refereed by officials wearing Prince Albert coats and high silk hats were played off the campus, taking advantage of facilities like those provided by the Minneapolis ball park. Then in 1899 the university acquired its own Northrop Field, and in 1923 it was replaced by Memorial Stadium, which was typical of the large arenas springing up on campuses throughout the nation at the time. Under the leadership of great coaches like Dr. H. L. Williams and Bernie Bierman, Minnesota has produced some championship teams and numerous all-American players.

Not only at the university, but in various other Minnesota schools and colleges, student athletes have attained a high degree of skill in such sports as track, baseball, basketball, and hockey. Admissions for school sports competitions purchased by Minnesotans in 1949 totaled more than four million, and professional events in the state drew almost as many spectators in the same year.

Thousands of the state's citizens engage in participating sports like gymnastics, skiing, skating, tennis, golf, hunting, swimming, fishing, canoeing, iceboating, motorboating, and surfboard riding. The popularity of water sports is only natural in a state where ninety-five per cent of the people live within five miles of a lake or stream. The ever-growing number of Minnesotans who depend on industry for their livelihood enjoy easy access to the safety valve of outdoor recreation.

THE WILLIAMS HOUSE at White Bear Lake, erected in 1871, and its adjoining cottages could accommodate a hundred guests. *Photograph by Illingworth, about 1880.*

FRONTENAC'S Lake Side Hotel overlooked Lake Pepin with its dramatic scenery and steamboat traffic when Whitney took this photograph in the late 1860s.

THE HOTEL LAFAYETTE, the largest and most pretentious resort on Lake Minnetonka, was erected in 1882 by James J. Hill's railroad after its line was completed to Minnetonka Beach. *Lithograph, 1880s.*

COMMUTING transformed resort life after railroads reached some of Minnesota's beauty spots. These summer residents of Lindstrom, on a spur of the Northern Pacific, were waiting for the evening train from the Twin Cities. *Photograph by Dunn, 1913.*

LUTSEN RESORT, at the mouth of the Poplar River, has been a mecca for tourists seeking recreation on the beautiful north shore of Lake Superior since 1887, when the first lodge was built on the site. At that time, vacationers could reach the area by boat only. The lodge pictured below was built in 1952. *Courtesy Minnesota Division of Publicity.*

SWIMMING AND WADING were enjoyed by youngsters who went to Wildwood Park on White Bear Lake for outings, as well as by those vacationing at resorts. *Photograph taken about 1905.*

FISHING was excellent in Minnesota's northern lakes in 1896, when these disciples of Isaac Walton went to Leech Lake via the Northern Pacific Railroad and landed the big catch here displayed in an hour and a half. *Photograph by Bromley.*

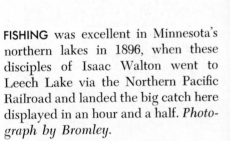

THE WILDERNESS AREA of northeastern Minnesota is a paradise for those who, like these tourists of 1941, enjoy camping and canoeing. *Courtesy Minnesota Division of Publicity.*

THE PICTURE ROCKS of Lac la Croix, with their aboriginal paintings of animals, birds, and other figures, are among the attractions of the famed canoe country along the international border from Lake Superior to Lake of the Woods. *Photograph by George M. Ryan.*

AT THE SOURCE OF THE FATHER OF WATERS modern tourists find this informative marker. Near by are steppingstones on which they can make their way across the infant stream as it leaves Lake Itasca. *Photograph by Dobie, 1951.*

LAKE ITASCA, as seen from Douglas Lodge, is typical of beautiful Itasca State Park, a forested area of nearly 32,000 acres dotted with 157 lakes. *Photograph by Donald C. Holmquist, 1955.*

DAN PATCH, who was considered the greatest pacer of all time, attracted record-breaking crowds to the Minnesota State Fair. *Photograph by Sweet Studios, 1908.*

THE FOOTBALL TEAM of the University of Minnesota was captained in 1887 by Alfred F. Pillsbury, third from the right in the lower row. Also in the group pictured, standing third from the right in the top row, is Walter ("Pudge") Heffelfinger, who went to Yale a year later.

SHATTUCK SCHOOL at Faribault had a championship track team in 1889.

BASEBALL fans flocked to Lexington Park on University Avenue in St. Paul when that field was the home of the locally owned "Saints." *Photograph probably taken in the 1920s.*

BASEBALL CLUBS sponsored by some of Minnesota's smaller communities included the state championship team of 1901 from Waseca. *Courtesy Waseca County Historical Society, Waseca.*

IN MEMORIAL STADIUM, the University of Minnesota football teams play their home games before crowds that total more than 63,000 when the arena is filled. *Photograph taken in 1957; courtesy University Department of Physical Education.*

25.

Political Maverick

POLITICALLY, Minnesota was characterized by a reporter in the *New York Times* of March 26, 1956, as "one of the most independent and unpredictable of states in the Union." This comment, inspired by Senator Estes Kefauver's victory on the Democratic ticket in the Minnesota presidential primary of 1956, describes fittingly much of the state's long record as a political maverick.

True, throughout the first forty years of statehood, Minnesota seemed to conform to the pattern that dominated Midwest politics. Following the initial Democratic administration of 1858, the voters consistently gave pluralities to Republican governors until 1898 and to Republican presidents until 1912. Furthermore, most of the governors of the period were Civil War veterans. In naming chief executives like Stephen Miller, William R. Marshall, and Lucius F. Hubbard, Minnesota appeared to be following the example set by other states that had supported the Union cause. Beneath the surface of apparent conformity, however, forces were stirring that eventually shaped Minnesota's unique political future. They emerged as protest groups and third parties which voiced the agrarian discontent of an era of falling grain prices and economic distress for the farmer. The resulting "agrarian crusade" began with the organization of the National Grange of the Patrons of Husbandry in 1867 and was continued in successive decades before 1900 by the Anti-Monopoly and Greenback parties, the Farmers' Alliance, and the Populists.

Minnesotans figured prominently in these movements both on the local and the national front. Among them was Oliver H. Kelley, a farmer from Elk River who founded the Grange. His success in his home state can be judged from the fact that by 1874 Minnesota could claim more than five hundred of the nation's twenty thousand granges —farmers' clubs working to advance the cause of agriculture through education. Although the Grange was a nonpolitical secret order, it successfully influenced legislation in favor of the interests it supported. As a result, its members realized that farmers as a group were capable of independent political action. That came under the leadership of another Minnesotan, Ignatius Donnelly, who had served as a Republican lieutenant governor and congressman during much of the decade following 1859. Eventually he bolted the party, became an independent, participated in Grange affairs, and, in 1873, began to engage in third-party political activity. With his assistance, the Farmers' Alliance was launched at Chicago in 1880 and the People's party or Populist movement was organized at Cincinnati in 1891. In Minnesota, first the Alliance and then the Populists gained virtual control of the legislature both in 1890 and 1892. Such displays of strength earned the respect of governors and legislators, who began to enact some of the farmers' demands into law. The Populists' attempt in 1892 to make Donnelly Minnesota's chief executive, however, ended in failure. He was decisively defeated by Knute Nelson, a liberal Republican of Norwegian descent, who adopted many Populist policies and won the support of large groups of farmers. He was the first of a long line of Minnesota governors of Scandinavian birth or ancestry.

Evidence that increasing Populist strength was causing alarm among Republicans is to be found in the selection of Minneapolis for the Republican national convention of 1892. The GOP had lost every Minnesota Congressional district except one in the election of 1890, and it hoped to retrieve its prestige in the state by selecting its presidential candidate in the Midwestern hotbed of agrarian unrest. The eighteen hundred delegates who assembled for the Mill City convention on June 7, 1892, nominated Benjamin Harrison for re-election. Although he carried Minnesota, the president was defeated by a Democrat, Grover Cleveland, in the November election.

It was another Democrat, John Lind, who in 1898 finally won a governorship for Minnesota's third-party forces. His name was placed on the state ticket as a fusion candidate, supported by Democrats, Populists, and Silver Republicans, all of whom favored the free silver policy of William Jennings Bryan, Democratic nominee for the presidency. Lind's victory marked the first state-wide success of Minnesota's independent voters—a triumph that had its roots deep in the agrarian discontent of the 1870s and 1880s. Although this "oracle of progressive and independent thought" was defeated in 1900 by Republican Samuel R. Van Sant, a second Democrat soon succeeded to the chief executive's post. He was John A. Johnson, the first native Minnesotan to serve his state as governor. A son of Swedish immigrants who was reared in poverty near St. Peter, Johnson was a magnetic leader of great personal popularity. His appeal for the electorate was so great that he again won the governorship in 1904, a presidential year which in Minnesota was marked by a Republican landslide for Theodore Roosevelt. After being twice re-elected and drawing national attention as a presidential possibility, Johnson died suddenly in September, 1909.

A Republican regime of twenty years, broken only by Winfield S. Hammond's brief Democratic term in 1915, followed Johnson's death. First among the era's four Republican governors was A. O. Eberhart, a native of Sweden who was Minnesota's last foreign-born chief executive. During his administration, in 1913, the Minnesota legislature

AT GRANGE MEETINGS, like this one of 1873 in Illinois, speakers urged members to demand "Free Trade and Farmers' Rights" and to "Organize and Educate, for Knowledge is Power." *From* Leslie's Illustrated Newspaper, *August 30, 1873; courtesy Library of Congress.*

IGNATIUS DONNELLY, a stirring orator, served as a leader of the third-party movements of the 1870s, 1880s, and 1890s. *Photograph by Charles A. Zimmerman, about 1890.*

DONNELLY complained loudly in 1894 about "the political party I have done so much to create" after the Populists nominated Sidney M. Owen for the Minnesota governorship. The situation was satirized by Flloyd W. Triggs in this cartoon published in the *Minneapolis Tribune, August 31, 1894.*

KNUTE NELSON went to the United States Senate in 1895, serving there longer than any other Minnesotan. His term ended only with his death in 1923. *Photograph by Trenham, about 1880.*

JOHN LIND, pictured below in his office in the old Capitol, was the first Democratic leader to be elected to the Minnesota governorship after the Civil War. *Photograph taken about 1900.*

JOHN A. JOHNSON (right) and Henry J. Essler are shown below in the office of the *St. Peter Herald,* which they edited and published as partners after 1886. Essler encouraged Johnson's participation in Democratic politics which resulted in his election as governor in 1904. *Courtesy Nicollet County Historical Society.*

IN THE GUBERNATORIAL RACE of 1912, Republican Eberhart defeated his Democratic and Progressive opponents. *Cartoon by Matthew T. Caine, in the* St. Paul Pioneer Press, *September 22, 1912.*

ARTHUR C. TOWNLEY (left), founder of the Nonpartisan League, personally organized farmers for political action. *Courtesy* St. Paul Dispatch-Pioneer Press.

NONPARTISAN LEAGUE organizers, like the one pictured below speaking in Carver County, campaigned for Lindbergh for governor in 1918.

MAGNUS JOHNSON (above), a Meeker County farmer who had served earlier in the state legislature, was elected to the United States Senate on a Farmer-Labor ticket in 1923. *Photograph by Kenneth M. Wright Studios.*

GOVERNOR OLSON (right) and Senator Shipstead, pictured in the former's office, were leaders of the Farmer-Labor regime of the 1930s. *Photograph probably taken about 1932.*

took on the nonpartisan character which has since distinguished it from all other state lawmaking bodies except that of Nebraska. In 1920, midway in the post-Johnson era, women voted for the first time for president and governor, adding substantially to the pluralities of Warren G. Harding and J. A. O. Preus. The two decades of Republican rule were not unmarked, however, by evidences of Minnesota's political independence. The election of 1912, when Minnesotans approved Theodore Roosevelt's insurgent Progressive party at the polls, provides an example. In that year, for the first time, the state turned its back on a Republican candidate for the presidency.

The century's second decade was marked, too, by the birth of a new political party, which, like earlier movements, stemmed from agrarian discontent. The original organization, known as the Nonpartisan League, developed in North Dakota under the leadership of Arthur C. Townley. The "political prairie fire" he kindled spread into Minnesota's

268

western counties by 1916, and within two years it acquired enough strength to participate in politics in the North Star State. After failing in an attempt to nominate Charles A. Lindbergh, Sr., for the governorship as a Republican in 1918, the league decided to name its own ticket, and to satisfy legal requirements it adopted the name "Farmer-Labor party" for use on the ballots. Its showing in the election that followed was impressive, its candidate, David H. Evans, polling almost 112,000 votes to Republican J. A. A. Burnquist's 166,515.

Although the First World War retarded the development of the new political group, the combined labor and agricultural interests sent two senators to Washington in the 1920s. Henrik Shipstead was elected in 1922, and a year later Magnus Johnson succeeded the veteran Knute Nelson, who died in office. Johnson merely filled out Nelson's term, but Shipstead continued to represent Minnesota—after 1940 as a Republican— in the United States Senate until 1947.

In the 1930s—the era of the great depression—the Farmer-Labor group emerged as a full-blown third party capable of controlling state politics. Floyd B. Olson became Minnesota's first Farmer-Labor governor in 1931, continuing in office until his death in 1936. He was followed by two fellow Farmer-Laborites. In the election of 1936 the party not only named most of Minnesota's state officials, but it gained control of the lower house of the legislature and captured both United States Senate seats and a majority of the Congressional posts.

Two years later, Minnesotans again demonstrated their political independence by electing Republican Harold E. Stassen to the governorship while giving support to the Democratic party nationally. Through three succeeding administrations the Republicans maintained their lead in the state, naming Edward J. Thye, Luther W. Youngdahl, and C. Elmer Anderson to the chief executive's chair. In the meantime, the Farmer-

GOVERNOR YOUNGDAHL and the Misses Anna E. R. and Laura Furness, granddaughters of Minnesota's first Republican governor, Alexander Ramsey, were photographed in 1949 in the Ramsey house in St. Paul. *Photograph by Hank Walker; courtesy Life and Time Inc., New York.*

THE REPUBLICAN NATIONAL CONVENTION of 1892 in Minneapolis was attended by 1,800 delegates from forty-four states and four territories. *From* Harper's Weekly, *June 11, 1892.*

DELEGATES who nominated Harrison entered the convention hall of the Minneapolis Exposition Building via this staircase. *Photograph taken June 7, 1892; courtesy Library of Congress.*

Labor party had fused with the Democrats in 1944, emerging as the Democratic-Farmer-Labor party. The new organization sent Hubert H. Humphrey to the United States Senate in 1949. Another major victory on the state level came in 1954 with the election of Orville L. Freeman to the governorship, a post to which he was again named in 1956.

Further evidence of Minnesota's political nonconformity is to be found in the state's presidential voting record since 1912, when it registered its first break with the Republican tradition. Following that event, Minnesota returned to the GOP fold, supporting four successive Republican candidates—Charles Evans Hughes, Warren G. Harding, Calvin Coolidge, and Herbert Hoover—between 1916 and 1928. Then in 1932, two years after the original Farmer-Labor victory on a state level, Minnesota for the first time gave its presidential approval to a Democrat, Franklin D. Roosevelt. He continued to carry the state through 1944, and his successor, Harry S. Truman, won Minnesota in 1948. After 1938 Republicans, however, were for sixteen years consistently elected to state offices. The voters again gave evidence of their penchant for nonconformity in the 1950s by supporting a Republican, President Dwight D. Eisenhower, while putting a Democratic-Farmer-Labor governor in the Capitol at St. Paul.

That this doubtful state has long been a center of intensive campaigning by presidents and presidential aspirants is not surprising. William Jennings Bryan courted Minnesota's farmers on their home territory in 1900 and again in 1908; President William H. Taft inaugurated his attempt to win Midwest support for the Republican protective tariff at Winona on September 17, 1909, thereby precipitating a split in his party that resulted in its defeat nationally both in 1910 and 1912; Hughes in 1916 and Theodore Roosevelt in 1918 campaigned in the state as Republicans opposed to President Woodrow Wilson and his objectives; both Hoover and Franklin Roosevelt delivered important

PRESIDENT HAYES spoke at the Northwestern Fair in Minneapolis (below) and at the State Fair in St. Paul in 1878, stressing financial problems that followed the panic of 1873. *From Harper's Weekly, October 5, 1878; courtesy St. Paul Public Library.*

CHARLES EVANS HUGHES carried Minnesota for the Republicans in 1916 by fewer than four hundred votes after touring the state in a campaign train which made this stop at Winona. Nationally, the election resulted in Wilson's second victory on the Democratic ticket.

campaign speeches in St. Paul in 1932; and the contestants of 1952 and 1956 made bids for Minnesota's farm and labor vote in tours that took them to both rural and urban centers. Among presidents who helped win support for their policies and parties on visits to Minnesota were Rutherford B. Hayes, who toured the state, spoke at its agricultural fairs, and viewed its bonanza farms in 1878; Chester A. Arthur, who attended the festivities that marked the completion of the Northern Pacific Railroad in 1883; William McKinley, who was on hand to welcome the Thirteenth Minnesota when it returned from Manila in 1899; and Coolidge, who participated in the Norse-American Centennial celebration at the state fairgrounds in St. Paul in 1925.

As his secretary of war from 1879 to 1881, President Hayes named Alexander Ramsey, the first governor of the territory, who thus achieved new honors by becoming the first resident of the state to sit in a president's cabinet. Other Minnesotans who held cabinet posts were William Windom, secretary of the treasury under Garfield in 1881 and under Harrison from 1889 to 1891; Frank B. Kellogg, Coolidge's secretary of state from

EX-PRESIDENT THEODORE ROOSEVELT addressed about four thousand workers in the war plant of the Minneapolis Steel and Machinery Company on October 7, 1918, advocating the election of Republican congressmen who would prevent President Wilson from shaping the peace.

1925 to 1929; and William D. Mitchell, attorney general in Hoover's cabinet from 1929 to 1933. Harold Stassen was given "cabinet rank" in 1955, when he was named by President Eisenhower as special assistant to direct studies of world disarmament. The state's lone Supreme Court justice was Pierce Butler, who served from 1923 to 1939.

Minnesotans who left their state for diplomatic posts abroad include Christopher C. Andrews, minister to Sweden and Norway from 1869 to 1877; Laurits S. Swenson, minister to four European countries; Kellogg, ambassador to Great Britain in 1924–25; Robert Butler, ambassador to Australia from 1946 to 1948; and Eugenie Anderson, ambassador to Denmark from 1949 to 1953. When Mrs. Anderson went from Red Wing to Copenhagen, she became the first American woman to represent her country with the rank of ambassador at a foreign court. These diverse personalities have colored Minnesota's contribution to national politics, while leaders like Ignatius Donnelly, Knute Nelson, John A. Johnson, Floyd B. Olson, and Harold Stassen—mavericks all when first they loomed on the political horizon—have given distinction to its record at home.

273

PRESIDENT EISENHOWER campaigned in Minnesota in 1952, speaking in communities like Northfield, where this photograph was taken on September 17. *Courtesy* St. Paul Dispatch-Pioneer Press.

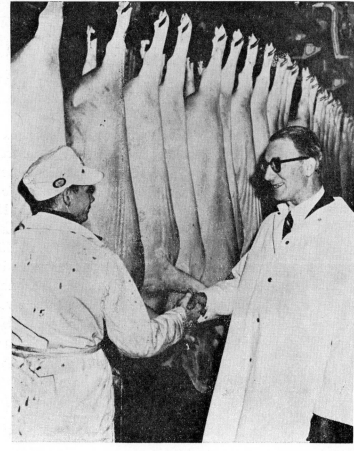

SENATOR ESTES KEFAUVER carried his campaign for the Democratic presidential nomination to Minnesota's workers in 1956. The picture at the right was taken on February 20 in the George A. Hormel packing plant at Austin. *Courtesy* St. Paul Dispatch-Pioneer Press.

WILLIAM WINDOM served as secretary of the treasury in the cabinets of two Republican presidents. *Photograph by Brady; courtesy National Archives.*

FRANK B. KELLOGG became Minnesota's most widely known statesman by serving in the 1920s as ambassador to Great Britain and as President Coolidge's secretary of state. This photograph, probably taken about 1926, shows him with President and Mrs. Coolidge and Mrs. Kellogg.

EUGENIE ANDERSON presented her ambassador's credentials to King Frederick IX of Denmark shortly before this picture was taken in the doorway of the palace in Copenhagen on December 22, 1949. *Courtesy Mrs. Anderson, Red Wing.*

26.

Minnesota
in Four Wars

WITH THE DECLARATION OF WAR on Spain, a peaceful era of more than three decades came to an abrupt close for Minnesota and the nation on April 25, 1898. War fever had been raging ever since the American battleship "Maine" sank in the harbor at Havana on February 15. Public opinion, aroused by that disaster, was stimulated by lurid newspaper reports of Spanish abuses and civil war in Cuba. Eventually, Congress interfered, passing joint resolutions which caused Spain to sever diplomatic relations with the United States. The federal call for volunteers which followed met with swift response in Minnesota. Three units of its National Guard assembled before the month ended, and early in May they were mustered into the service of the United States as the Twelfth, Thirteenth, and Fourteenth regiments of Minnesota Volunteers. The Fifteenth was organized in July in response to a second call for recruits. Minnesota was strongly represented, too, in some units of the regular army, notably the Third United States Infantry, which had been stationed at Fort Snelling since 1888.

Of the volunteer regiments, the Thirteenth, commanded by Colonel Charles M. Reeve, was the only one to see foreign service. It left St. Paul on May 16 and embarked at San Francisco for the Philippines on June 26. There the Minnesota unit participated in the battle of Manila, helped suppress a native insurrection, and served in various other military capacities for more than a year. Involved also in engagements with the revolting Filipinos was the Third Infantry, which left Fort Snelling in January, 1899, after crushing an Indian uprising at Leech Lake. The Thirteenth returned to the United States in the autumn of 1899, receiving enthusiastic welcomes in St. Paul and Minneapolis, where President McKinley and members of his cabinet were on hand to participate in the home-coming celebration. Less fortunate were the men of the Third Infantry; they remained in the Philippines until March, 1902, and thereafter they were stationed at various other American military posts for almost twenty years before their unit returned to Fort Snelling in November, 1921.

276

SOLDIERS of the Third United States Infantry left a snowy Fort Snelling by streetcar when they departed for overseas service in the tropical Philippines on January 30, 1899.

THE THIRTEENTH MINNESOTA, returning from the Philippines on October 12, 1899, passed in review before President McKinley, Governor Lind, and other notables who welcomed the regiment in Minneapolis. *Stereograph by Strohmeyer and Wyman; courtesy Library of Congress.*

In the intervening decades, Minnesotans once more had been called upon to serve their country overseas when the United States became involved in World War I. Within days after President Wilson's war resolution was approved by Congress on April 6, 1917, Minnesota's Naval Militia left Duluth for Philadelphia, and the National Guard was called into active service. Three infantry regiments went to Camp Cody, New Mexico, and the unit that had been known as the First Minnesota Field Artillery was ordered to Camp Mills, Long Island. There, as the 151st Field Artillery, it was assigned to the Forty-second or "Rainbow" Division of the American Expeditionary Force, which in France participated in some of the heaviest fighting of World War I. Its role in the war of 1917–18, under the command of Colonel George E. Leach, resembled that of the Thirteenth Minnesota in 1898–99, for the 151st became a symbol of the state's participation in the later conflict on foreign soil.

Upon mobilization, other state units lost their identity to a large degree, among them three that were absorbed by the Thirty-fourth Division. The thousands of Minnesotans who enlisted or were drafted after the departure of the National Guard served beside men from every state in the Union. Active recruiting stimulated enlistments from Minnesota and drew about forty thousand of its citizens into the army, navy, and marine corps. Nearly seventy-five thousand men ranging in age from twenty-one to forty-five, who registered under the Selective Service Act, were drafted from Minnesota. In all, the state contributed to the war the services of 118,000 individuals, including a thousand nurses.

While Minnesota's young men were engaged in overseas fighting, civilians were mobilizing at home to contribute to the war effort. The Minnesota Commission of Public Safety was set up to organize the state's resources; a home guard was established; some twenty thousand women joined a state-wide organization that engaged in various types of war activity; wheat and iron ore—vital ingredients of the war effort—were produced in larger quantities than ever before; the Red Cross organized 1,200 units in the state and enrolled half a million members who sewed, knitted, and in other ways provided for the fighting man's welfare; Minnesotans subscribed some $450,000,000 to four Liberty Loans and a Victory Loan; and the people of the state helped conserve resources by observing wheatless, meatless, and heatless days, lightless nights, and gasless Sundays.

For the first time, the life of every citizen was touched by a war. That its conclusion should be marked by a great outburst of spontaneous rejoicing was only natural. In the cities, whistles, bells, and chimes heralded the news of the armistice of November 11, 1918, and all work ceased as parading, dancing, singing, and shouting crowds filled the streets. According to a Minneapolis paper, the celebration there resembled "a thousand New Year Eves and Halloweens rolled into one." Those who believed the armistice would be quickly followed by the return of their loved ones were, however, disappointed. Not until May 8, 1919, did the 151st Field Artillery arrive in St. Paul, where a triumphal arch had been erected to honor the returning heroes, and it was even later

THE COLOR COMPANY of the Thirty-sixth United States Infantry, stationed at Fort Snelling, marched through the streets of St. Paul in July, 1917, to help stimulate enlistments. *Courtesy* St. Paul Dispatch-Pioneer Press.

DRAFTED MEN in groups like this one, photographed on their departure from White Bear Lake in the spring of 1918, left communities throughout the state en route to training centers which prepared them for service in World War I. *Courtesy* St. Paul Dispatch-Pioneer Press.

BOY SCOUTS participated in the Liberty Loan drives of the First World War by selling bonds on the streets of St. Paul in the spring of 1918. This booth, which featured a liberty bell and urged citizens to "ring it again" by buying their quota of bonds, was on the corner of Sixth and Robert streets. *Courtesy* St. Paul Dispatch-Pioneer Press.

RED CROSS WORKERS, like the St. Paul group pictured below, produced surgical dressings for use in field hospitals during World War I. *Photograph probably taken in 1917.*

CANTEEN WORKERS for the American Red Cross assisted soldiers passing through Minnesota on troop trains. *Photograph taken at the St. Paul Union Depot, probably in 1918.*

THE ARMISTICE of November 11, 1918, was celebrated in Minneapolis by jubilant crowds that gathered on Nicollet Avenue.

THE 151ST FIELD ARTILLERY returned to Minnesota on May 8, 1919, receiving an enthusiastic welcome in St. Paul as it paraded on Sixth Street, which was spanned by a triumphal arch at Wabasha. *Courtesy* St. Paul Dispatch-Pioneer Press.

FORT SNELLING was used as a reception center in World War II. The bayonet drill pictured above was part of the basic training course given at the pioneer Minnesota military post. *Photograph taken in September, 1942; courtesy* St. Paul Dispatch-Pioneer Press.

FORT SNELLING'S language school of World War II employed many Nisei, who trained linguists for service in the Pacific theater of war. *Photograph taken in October, 1945; courtesy* St. Paul Dispatch-Pioneer Press.

DRAFTED MEN who reported for service at the St. Paul Armory during World War II left for induction centers by truck. *Photograph taken in July, 1943; courtesy* St. Paul Dispatch-Pioneer Press.

in the year before remnants of the Minnesota units in the Thirty-fourth Division were back in their home state.

With the Japanese attack on Pearl Harbor on December 7, 1941, the nation once more became involved in a world war. Four days later, the United States entered the war in a second theater in Europe, where the conflict had been raging for more than two years. Both the state and the nation were better prepared than in 1917. The first peacetime conscription in American history, which began after the Selective Training and Service Act became law in September, 1940, drew thousands of Minnesotans into the nation's armed forces before hostilities opened, and eighteen units of the Minnesota National Guard were mustered into the federal service in 1940 and early in 1941. Included was the 151st Field Artillery of World War I fame. Most of the Minnesota units were absorbed by the Thirty-fourth Division, which, after a period of strenuous training in Louisiana, was sent abroad in February, 1942.

In the months and years that followed, Minnesotans were involved in dramatic and decisive action in such far-flung sections of the globe as the Philippines, North Africa, Italy, the Aleutians, and the Normandy beaches of France. Among special units activated at Fort Snelling was the 704th Division of the Military Railway Service, sponsored by the Great Northern Railroad. Between November, 1942, and July, 1945, it saw service under the command of Brigadier General Carl R. Gray in North Africa, Italy, France, and Germany. During the five years that followed the first application of the Selective Service Act in 1940, no fewer than 186,704 residents of Minnesota were inducted into the various armed services through the draft, and 102,957 of the state's men and women enlisted. Out of the total figure, 7,936 never returned.

Like its military participation in the conflict of 1941–45, the state's civilian contribution was far more extensive and varied than it had been in World War I. Once more the United States and its allies looked to Minnesota for food and iron. In response, the state greatly increased its grain, flour, and livestock production; and it furnished about two-thirds of the iron ore used by American steel mills. In the field of industry, this once largely agricultural state made its most impressive contribution to the war effort. Plants throughout the area operated day and night to meet the quotas specified in government contracts, with men and women working side by side on shifts that continued around the clock. The Twin Cities Ordnance Plant at New Brighton manufactured ammunition, turning out cartridges by the millions, and the Gopher Ordnance Plant at Rosemount was established for the production of smokeless powder. A firm at Owatonna which normally manufactured jewelry turned to the production of bombsights; the St. Paul branch of a firm that made harvesters concentrated on automatic aircraft guns; a Minneapolis manufacturer of heat regulators made equipment for tanks and airplanes; a maker of pumps at Fridley filled contracts for gun mounts used by the navy; some of the larger structures on the state fairgrounds in St. Paul housed a plant that produced airplane propellers; pulpwood from International Falls was transformed into structural board for use in prefabricated huts built for the army at Bayport. Most surprising of all were the ships produced for the war effort in a state so far removed from every seaboard. In the very center of the North American continent, ocean-going vessels were constructed, largely at Duluth and Savage. About a hundred and fifty craft completed by two Duluth firms reached salt water via the Great Lakes and the St. Lawrence during the war years, and scores of barges and tankers built at Savage floated down the Mississippi to New Orleans after being launched on the Minnesota River.

Once more civilians were called upon to conserve materials essential to the war effort. In sharp contrast to the voluntary methods of World War I was the highly organized rationing system of the 1940s, developed by the Office of Price Administration. Every individual became conscious of shortages as automobile tires, the first item to be rationed, were followed by gasoline, sugar, coffee, shoes, processed foods, meat, and dozens of other essential commodities. The work of the OPA in Minnesota was much like its operation in every other part of the nation. The state made a special contribution to the wartime food picture, however, through its university, where a study of starvation resulted in the development of the emergency K ration used thereafter by the armed forces. The university also trained some of the physicists who did pioneering work in atomic research, and its Cadet Nurse Corps program probably enrolled more student nurses than that of any other American institution.

The close of World War II, marked by the German and Japanese surrenders of May

THE NAVY TANKER "Agawam," the first built in the wartime shipyards at Savage on the Minnesota River, passed St. Paul on November 5, 1943, on its way down the Mississippi. *Photograph taken in 1943; courtesy* St. Paul Dispatch-Pioneer Press.

THE LAST RETREAT AT FORT SNELLING was marked by the lowering of Old Glory on October 14, 1946, a few hours before the post was turned over to the Veterans' Administration.

7 and August 14, 1945, brought no such spontaneous outburst of joy as did the armistice of 1918. Once more Minnesotans slowly made their way home, this time to a state sobered by four years of war. Within five years they were again called upon to help fight a war in the Pacific. During the Korean conflict which began on June 27, 1950, some 95,000 Minnesotans served in the armed forces, and 10,000 participated in active fighting in Korea.

In the three conflicts that began in 1898, 1917, and 1941, the old stone fort that had been guarding the junction of the Mississippi and the Minnesota since 1819 played an important role. Many of the Minnesotans who served in the war with Spain were mustered in and trained at Fort Snelling. During World War I, a school for officers was among the military projects located there. The numerous undertakings centering at the Minnesota post during World War II included a Military Intelligence Service Language School which trained six thousand interpreters in Japanese, Korean, and Chinese for service in the Pacific. Among both instructors and students were hundreds of Nisei —persons of Japanese ancestry—who had been removed from their former homes in the Pacific coast area. Many Nisei also were trained for combat at Fort Snelling and attached to the Thirty-fourth Division.

Although some air force and other units used the Minnesota fort's facilities during and after the Korean War, the old post had been retired from active military service following the close of World War II. At midnight on October 14, 1946, the Veterans' Administration took over at the fort. The close of its military career was marked by a ceremony at 5:00 P.M., when the flag in front of the headquarters building was lowered in a final retreat. Today Fort Snelling's gray stone Round Tower and other ancient structures serve as reminders of Minnesota's participation in the Civil War as well as in four later conflicts on foreign shores.

27.

Centennial Contrasts

ANNIVERSARIES provide an occasion for taking stock, for measuring the progress made over a span of years. Minnesota's statehood centennial falls naturally into this pattern. The event gives the people of the commonwealth an opportunity to pause and survey its evolution, particularly since its admission to the Union in 1858. Statistics furnish one measure of the state's development in the past hundred years, albeit a cold and lifeless one. A warmer and more vivid reflection of the changes wrought by a century is mirrored in the pictures which bring this unconventional history to a close—a half dozen scenes familiar to most Minnesotans of the 1950s with contrasting visual records made four to ten decades earlier.

THE CAPITOL APPROACH, 1957. Wide boulevards lead to Cass Gilbert's gleaming marble statehouse and the office buildings which surround it. *Aerial photograph by Walter H. Wettschreck.*

THE CAPITOL APPROACH, 1857. An ugly frontier village of irregular muddy streets, ramshackle frame houses, and simple churches surrounded the territorial Capitol in St. Paul on the eve of state-hood. *Photograph by Upton.*

THE SITE OF MINNEAPOLIS, 1854. When this daguerreotype was taken, Sioux Indians were encamped at what became Bridge Square, near the west end of the Hennepin Avenue Bridge. In the background is the house of John H. Stevens, the first in the future city.

BRIDGE SQUARE, 1873. The area was used as a public market where farmers sold produce, and the City Hall had just been built on the adjoining tract bounded by Hennepin and Nicollet avenues and Second Street. *Courtesy Minneapolis Public Library.*

BRIDGE SQUARE, ABOUT 1900. Horse-drawn vehicles and streetcars moved in city traffic where Indians had pitched their tipis less than fifty years earlier. *Photograph by Bromley; courtesy Minneapolis Public Library.*

MINNEAPOLIS IN THE 1950s. The identity of Bridge Square is lost in the maze of a great city. *Courtesy Minneapolis Chamber of Commerce.*

DULUTH AND MINNESOTA POINT, ABOUT 1870. Pioneers who viewed the infant city from the heights above Lake Superior saw a water front served by a single dock and outlined by flimsy wooden buildings. *Photograph by Zimmerman.*

DULUTH AND MINNESOTA POINT, 1952. A ship canal pierces the narrow peninsula, providing a convenient approach to a great fresh-water harbor dominated by grain elevators and ore docks. *Photograph by Gallagher's Studio; courtesy Duluth Chamber of Commerce.*

MAIN STREET, SAUK CENTRE, 1877.
This newly incorporated Stearns County village was typical of the rural communities that grew up as settlers and railroads penetrated central and western Minnesota in the decade of the 1870s.

MAIN STREET, SAUK CENTRE, 1957. A symbol of main streets throughout America, this Minnesota thoroughfare is dominated by a movie theater named for the novel that made the community famous. *Photograph by Lee Hanley; courtesy Father Colman Barry, Collegeville.*

THE MAYO CLINIC, ROCHESTER, 1913. This building was the early home of the medical center which became a mecca for ailing humanity. *Courtesy Olmsted County Historical Society.*

THE MAYO CLINIC, ROCHESTER, 1955. One of Minnesota's most important institutions occupies this modern building, which is its third home. In the rear is its second, now the Plummer Building, built in 1929. *Courtesy Minnesota Division of Publicity.*

THE MINNESOTA STATE FAIR, 1860. Fort Snelling provided the buildings and grounds for this pioneer agricultural exhibition. *Photograph by Upton.*

THE MINNESOTA STATE FAIR, 1955. This vast annual exhibition — the largest of its kind in the nation — reflects the state's agricultural growth during the course of a century. *Courtesy* St. Paul Dispatch-Pioneer Press.

Picture Sources

OF THE 477 illustrations in this book, 285 were selected from the more than 450,000 oil paintings, water colors, prints, daguerreotypes, and photographs owned by the Minnesota Historical Society. The remaining 192 items presented in the volume were found in private hands and in collections located in many parts of the United States, Canada, and Europe. For their use the author is indebted to 18 individuals and 66 museums, libraries, schools, state and county historical societies, governmental agencies and departments, business firms, newspapers, and the like. A credit line accompanies every picture that comes from a source other than the Minnesota Historical Society; all items without credit lines are from the latter's collection. The names of contributing agencies and individuals given in the list that follows have been omitted from the index.

American Museum of Natural History, New York City

Mrs. Andrew G. Anderson, Hibbing

Mrs. Eugenie Anderson, Red Wing

Richard H. Anderson, Big Fork

Father Colman Barry, Collegeville

Miss Edith L. Beardsley, Hibbing

Beltrami County Historical Society, Bemidji

Charles J. Brown, Marine-on-St. Croix

Bureau of American Ethnology, Smithsonian Institution, Washington, D.C.

Canada Steamship Lines, William H. Coverdale Collection, Montreal

Chicago Historical Society, Chicago

Clay County Historical Society, Moorhead

Cold Spring Granite Company, Cold Spring

Crow Wing County Courthouse, Brainerd

Mrs. George S. Currie, Westmount, Quebec

John Dobie, St. Paul

Dodge County Historical Society, Mantorville

Duluth Chamber of Commerce

James Taylor Dunn, St. Paul

Eastern National Park and Monument Association, Philadelphia

George Eastman House, Rochester, New York

Faribault County Historical Society, Blue Earth

Misses Anna E. R. and Laura Furness, St. Paul

Mrs. F. W. Gerber, Plainview

Thomas Gilcrease Institute of American History and Art, Tulsa

Goucher College, Baltimore

Miss Gertrude Gove, St. Cloud

Great Northern Railway Company, St. Paul

J. E. Haynes, Bozeman, Montana

Lieutenant Colonel S. A. Heward, Toronto
James Jerome Hill Reference Library, St. Paul
Hudson's Bay Company, Winnipeg
Lac qui Parle County Historical Society, Madison
Landesmuseum, Linz, Austria
Library of Congress, Washington, D.C.
Life and Time, Incorporated, New York City
Mrs. James Lumex, Le Center
McCord National Museum, McGill University, Montreal
Harold McCracken, Douglaston, Long Island, New York
Magney, Tusler, and Setter, Minneapolis
Maryland Historical Society, Baltimore
Minneapolis Aquatennial
Minneapolis Chamber of Commerce
Minneapolis Institute of Arts
Minneapolis Public Library
Minneapolis Sunday Tribune
Minnesota Arrowhead Association, Duluth
Minnesota Department of Conservation, St. Paul
Minnesota Division of Public Property, St. Paul
Minnesota Division of Publicity, St. Paul
Minnesota Highway Department, St. Paul
Minnesota State Archives Commission, St. Paul
Minnesota State Automobile Association, Minneapolis
National Archives, Washington, D.C.
National Museum, Smithsonian Institution, Washington, D.C.
Newberry Library, Chicago
New York Public Library, New York City

New York State Historical Association, Cooperstown
Nicollet County Historical Society, St. Peter
Northwest Airlines, St. Paul
Olmsted County Historical Society, Rochester
Ontario Department of Public Records and Archives, Toronto
Pine County Historical Society, Pine City
Public Archives of Canada, Ottawa
Public Archives of Manitoba, Winnipeg
Red Wing Potteries, Red Wing
Reserve Mining Company, Duluth
St. Benedict's Convent, St. Joseph
St. Louis County Historical Society, Duluth
St. Paul Dispatch-Pioneer Press, St. Paul
St. Paul Public Library
St. Paul Seminary, St. Paul
Sauk Centre Public Library, Sauk Centre
Sibley House Association, Minnesota Daughters of the American Revolution, Mendota
South Dakota State Historical Society, Pierre
State Historical Society of North Dakota, Bismarck
State Historical Society of Wisconsin, Madison
Hulbert Taft, Cincinnati
United States Military Academy, West Point
University of Minnesota, Agricultural Extension Service, St. Paul, and the Department of Physical Education, Minneapolis
Waseca County Historical Society, Waseca
Washington County Historical Society, Stillwater
Winona County Historical Society, Winona

Index

297

The Thirty-second State

is set in Caledonia, a Linotype face designed by W. A. Dwiggins. The text type is eleven point leaded three points, and the captions are ten point leaded two points. The introductory phrase in each caption is set in Spartan medium. Chapter headings are thirty-six point italic Bulmer.

The book was designed by Edmund M. Kopietz assisted by Alan Ominsky. It was composed, printed and bound by the North Central Publishing Company, St. Paul, Minnesota. The paper was manufactured by the Appleton Coated Paper Company, Appleton, Wisconsin.